Coaching in Th

CW01659273

A CIP catalog record for this book is available from the British Library.

Published by: Independent Publishing Network
First published in Great Britain 2018.
ISBN: 978-1-78926-847-8Author: John Borland
Distributor: Amazon - www.amazon.co.uk

Please direct all book orders or enquiries to the Distributor.

Coaching in The Great Unknown

Why not knowing matters more than you know

John Borland

Independent Publishing Network

About the Author

John Borland is a highly respected coach, trainer and speaker. He is an Accredited Master Coach and the co-founder and director of Fluent Coaching, a thriving coaching business in the north of England. He has spent the last decade coaching and training a wide range of people, from children to Chief Executives, and everyone in between. He has coached in education, business, charities, a range of public sector organisations and with hundreds of individual clients. He's the creator of the BRIGHT Coaching Framework and is outrageously passionate about helping people understand what coaching really is and how it positively impacts lives. He lives in the centre of a village with his wife Rachel and their three kids. If you search him on Wikipedia it will only reference his brief professional football career. This is his first book but probably not his last.

John can be contacted via email at **john@fluentcoaching.com** or online at **www.fluentcoaching.com**

Contents

Introduction

The Birth of a Book

Here I am at the beginning of the book I was never going to write. I don't know why, but throughout the course of my life I often end up doing the thing that years previously, I declared I would never do. This is how things tend to go for me. I've lost count of the amount of times I said I'd never write a book. For a very long time I didn't want to write a book, and then when I did, it took me an even longer time to finish. I suppose that's because some books are written when an author has a great idea they feel compelled to put on paper or perhaps the motivation comes through the kudos it will add to their career, or maybe it's simply for financial gain or recognition within a field. This book though, wasn't born for any of the above reasons. This book began life not inside of me, but in the requests and desires of other people. They were the brave souls who attended my training courses or talks, who would wander up to me at the end, ask whether I had a book and look slightly disappointed when I told them I had no intention of ever writing one. So, the beginnings of this book lie with all those people who asked me, told me and encouraged me to write down what I know about coaching, rather than just talk about it. I'm grateful to each of them. Even though this book has been dragged out of me, kicking and screaming at times, flowing and streaming at others, if you played a part in delivering that message to me, I am thankful that you did. Sorry, if at the time, I was stubbornly looking like I was rejecting the idea.

The Point

The whole point of this book is to help you understand the essence of coaching - what it really is and why it matters. I've been coaching professionally for over a decade now and working with the most eclectic range of people imaginable. I've taken coaching into places it has never been used before, from inner-city schools to executive board rooms, from the unemployed to millionaires. With every man, woman and child I have coached and trained, I have gathered a plethora of thoughts and ideas on coaching and how it really works. I've taken all these ideas and over the years developed something I suppose could be considered a coaching philosophy, which is more of an attitude and way of being with people, than any kind of systematic process. If you are new to coaching and wanting to understand how you too can be a coach, or use coaching within your role, then this book is for you. If you are already a coach and just wanting to perhaps gain a fresh perspective on coaching, then this book is also for you. I hope within its pages you find what you are looking for.

What to Expect

I haven't written everything I know about coaching, just the parts I think are most useful to support you in your coaching journey. There are some elements I have omitted, because I know they will be covered in whichever training you have done or decide to do as a coach, so for example, you'll find nothing in here about the functional operations of coaching or the ethical practices, like contracting or codes of conduct. You can find those elsewhere. This is a book about the essence of coaching, the heartbeat, the elements that really empower people to grow and in part it's about my journey from 'coaching sceptic' to master coach. All the theory within this book, whether it's mine or other people's, has emerged out of practice. I suppose it's a book that has been gradually etched, year on year inside my head and my heart, as I've understood more clearly what really does and doesn't make a difference to people.

The Coaching Parts

My philosophy of coaching has developed into five parts: the Unknowing; the Pillars; the Positions; the Skills and the Framework.

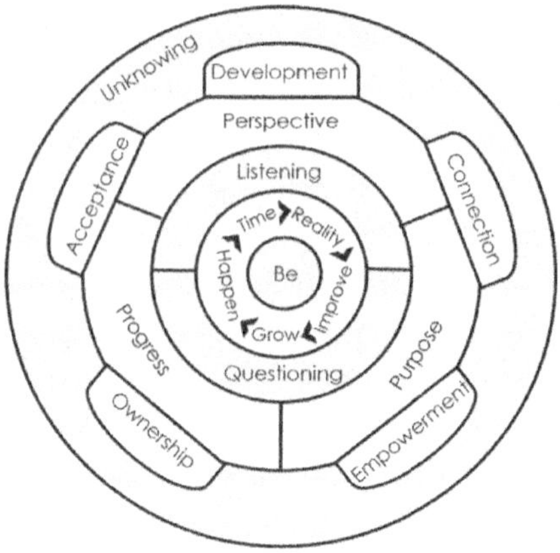

The Unknowing is simply the attitude that all coaches need; the Pillars are the foundations on which coaching must be built, they are Development, Connection, Empowerment, Ownership, and Acceptance.

The Three Positions give the coaching a holistic nature which enables people to expand their understanding and development, they are Perspective Coaching, Purpose Coaching and Progress Coaching.

The Two Skills of Coaching are Listening and Questioning, which sound straight forward enough but require great artistry to truly master.

The BRIGHT Coaching Framework gives coaches a place to begin and a way to make sense of coaching conversations which consists of Be, Reality, Improve, Grow, Happen and Time.

Once we've explored what coaching really is, we'll then look at each of these components of coaching and discover how and why they play their part in helping people. We'll also be 'standing on the shoulders of giants' throughout this whole process. I don't believe in reinventing wheels that are already rolling well, so I'll be mentioning other people and theories and how their ideas have a huge part to play in the coaching process. Learning to coach can be a scary business, it often takes a whole mindset shift to achieve, so please be open to ideas that may challenge your thinking and fly in the face of the way you have done things up to now. I hope this book stretches you, inspires you and at times irks you in the same way it has done for me over the years of writing it.

Chapter 1

It's Not Coaching

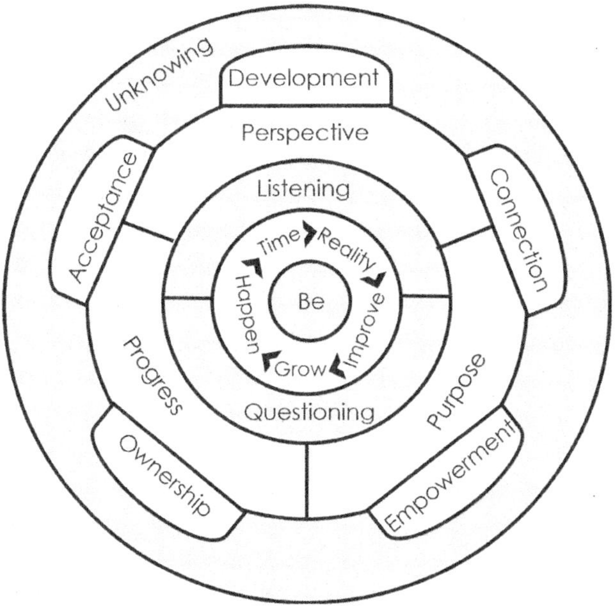

"We're all islands shouting lies to each other across seas of misunderstanding."

Rudyard Kipling, The Light That Failed

Coaching Beginnings

"Do you know anything about life coaching?" Isn't a question I imagine gets asked very often between two grown men, as the bell rings for last orders, in a scruffy, smoked-filled pub somewhere on the outskirts of a gritty northern city.

"Why are you asking?" came the response from Dermot, my flame bearded, deep-thinking Irish friend.

I shouldn't have been surprised, because in the decade I had known him he often answered my questions with a question. In previous years, this would have irritated me beyond belief, "Just answer the question" I would have been growling internally, yet I think he knew I needed to tell the story behind my question.

" I don't really know, it's just over the last few years or so, a few random people in various parts of my life, have told me they think I should be a life coach and I don't even know what the hell one of those is. It all sounds a bit wishy-washy, like fluffy-bunny stuff."

The first person to ever mention life coaching to me was Rob. We were just packing up after a youth club we had been running in an old converted church building we used as our youth centre. Sat right in the heart of one of the most deprived areas of inner-city Britain, this wasn't a lovely, picturesque youth club with beautifully behaved children, who all filed in and out perfectly, thanking us for the wonderful job we were doing. This was youth work on the edge, with kids who knew how to fight and scrap for everything in life. They were born and raised on housing estates into low-income families, with all manner of social barriers and obstacles to navigate. It was the kind of youth work where, as the doors opened, my adrenaline would start to rush, as I braced myself for what lay in store that night.

At first sight Rob had the appearance of a delicate man, slightly built with a greying beard, yet this did little to mask his outspoken, honest approach to life. If anyone displayed the proverbial "calling a spade a spade" it was Rob and I loved it about him.

"I think you should be a life coach," he said authoritatively.

"What the heck is one of those?" I threw straight back at him.

"I don't really know, but I think they help people improve their lives and you'd be really good at that," came a typical Rob reply.

And that's where it ended, my first ever conversation about coaching was three sentences long.

After my initial conversation with Rob, in that old church building, the thought of coaching never entered my conscious mind again until Sally, a work colleague, mentioned it about six months or so later. This was quickly followed by a man I got talking to at a conference; then a random friend of my parents; and some guy I heard on an American chat show.

Then, there I was, a year later, sat in that smoke-filled pub on the outskirts of Bradford asking Dermot if he could shed any light on the whole life coaching thing.

"How do you feel about being a life coach?" he asked.

"I don't know how I feel because I don't even know what life coaching is. It all sounds a bit weird and woolly to me, but when things keep cropping up in life in unrelated ways I always wonder if someone is trying to tell me something."

And then typically Dermot just throws into conversation, "I don't know a lot about it, but I do have a friend who's a life coach, I'm sure she could explain it a lot better than me."

He always has a friend who does something. Doesn't matter what you mention, he knows someone. The following week I made a phone call to Tiffany, the Life Coach and asked her to explain it to me. She did her best, but fifteen minutes into the phone call I realised that I simply didn't get it. I didn't really understand the crux of it. I could fathom the words she was speaking, but I had no idea what she really meant; how coaching worked or why it was even useful. I've come to understand now that I had no way of really getting to grips with what Tiffany was saying to me that day, because at the time I had no reference point for it. I had nothing to compare it to. It sounded a bit like counselling and a bit like mentoring, but I couldn't get any further than that. In order to make sense of it I knew I needed to experience it, so I asked her if I could have a coaching session.

I had no expectations, a nothingness. I couldn't even tell you I was nervous or excited before the coaching session with Tiffany because I had nothing to compare. There was just a vacuum, an empty space, but also a little part of me secretly hoping it was going to be a waste of time, so I could then put this whole coaching thing to bed and get on with my life.

It blew my mind! An hour of coaching with Tiffany was an experience I had never known before. It was a mixture of feeling more aware of myself than I had ever known, yet self-centered for talking solely about myself for an hour. It was the deepest, most useful conversation I had ever had, which was difficult to admit because it happened with a virtual stranger. But I was most certainly intrigued, and I needed to know more about this whole coaching thing.

What Coaching Isn't

Coaching is constantly confused with other practices. It is one of those baffling words that is familiar enough and yet slightly mysterious, at the same time. Therefore, it might sound back to front, but to understand what coaching is, we must first make sense of what coaching isn't. One of the difficulties of understanding coaching is that it's become such a buzz word in recent years. It can feel as though the whole world is calling themselves coaches, regardless of whether they are actually coaching or not. Maybe it sounds more user-friendly, or just cooler to carry the title coach, but there are hundreds of people out there, ranging from support workers to motivational speakers, who are all referring to themselves as coaches, when what they are doing isn't really coaching at all. The other big problem is coaching is regularly banded together with other similar practices, making it difficult to know exactly where coaching begins and ends. It is often confused with counselling, mentoring, training, leadership, motivational speaking, life skills programmes and a whole host of other things which muddy the waters when trying to truly understand coaching.

Most of the people I come across seem fairly certain they know what coaching is and yet in my experience, most don't, not really. The problem perpetuates because coaching is such a common word often associated with sports or business. Therefore, most of us have had some experience of someone calling themselves a coach, either a PE teacher back in school or a motivational speaker at a business event. To add to the confusion, if we don't really know what something is, we associate it with the closest thing we do know. It's like a food we have never tasted before, to make sense of what it tastes like, the best we can do is to associate it with something we already know. Which is why when I enquire about any new dish in a restaurant, the waiter's explanation of it is "it's a bit like chicken". It isn't like chicken at all, but I have nothing else to connect it with, I have no concept of it and therefore I have to understand it from the position of the closest thing I do know. Most people don't really know what coaching is, but what they do know is the next closest thing to it that they have some experience of. So, coaching is often thrown together with all these other practices that it's "a bit like".

Due to this ambiguity, we are going to briefly look at what sets coaching apart from some of its most common acquaintances. In no way am I claiming coaching is better or worse than any of the following, I just want us to be clear about the difference.

Coaching isn't Counselling

One of the frequent questions people who haven't come across coaching before ask is, "Is it a bit like counselling?" Coaching and counselling do share some common ground, in that if you were to observe a counselling session and a coaching session from a distance, they might look very similar. The setting may be comparable, as a one-on-one, confidential conversation where the client does most of the talking. The skills it takes to be a good coach, or a good counsellor can also be very transferable between either discipline. However, the real difference lies in the approach and focus of coaching and counselling. Put simply, counselling often focuses on the client's present thoughts and feelings and their past experiences. It aims to help them work through those experiences, in order to feel and think differently. Coaching, however, is not primarily focused on our client's past, but rather on their present reality and future progress and development. This doesn't mean we ban clients from talking about their past in coaching or that as coaches we are dismissive of our clients' back stories. Not at all, because they are a whole person who bring their past, present and future to our coaching relationship. It is simply that the focus is not on restoration from the past, but rather on forward development.

Coaching isn't mentoring

Coaching and mentoring are frequently joined together in training courses, development programmes and even in one of the major governing bodies, the European Council for Coaching & Mentoring. At first glance, it's understandable that coaching and mentoring do find themselves holding hands, because the intention and focus in both, is on the progress and development of the client. They are both present and future orientated and they both involve a relationship between two people. Yet, when we look more closely, the difference between the two is stark because of how the relationship and process is played out. A mentoring relationship involves a degree of hierarchy because it is held between an experienced mentor and a less experienced mentee, where the mentor guides the mentee using their own knowledge and experiences. For example, in a school, an experienced, skilled teacher would mentor a newly qualified teacher through the early years of their career. The mentor would use their own experiences as a guide to feedback to their mentee some advice and direction that will help them to develop in their career. In a coaching relationship there is absolutely no sense of this hierarchy. The coach doesn't guide the client from their own knowledge and experiences, rather they empower the client to discover for themselves their own path forward. A mentor tends to be someone who is ahead of their mentee in whatever walk of life or field of expertise the mentoring is taking place in. In coaching the coach is not in any way ahead of the client, in fact they are very much side by side with their client. There is no sense of hierarchy in coaching, as it is the client who is the expert in the room, because they are the only person who has lived their life though their eyes and therefore the only person who really understands their situation.

Coaching isn't Therapy

Therapy by its very nature, involves the healing and rehabilitation of a client in some way. A client may access therapy because they feel as though some part of them (either physically in the case of physiotherapy or mentally in the case of psychotherapy) needs some degree of restoration. In coaching there is no sense for the need of healing or rehabilitation for the client. Coaching starts at the point of the client recognising that they are OK exactly as they are and yet there is also vast scope for growth and development in themselves. This is vitally important, because many people who call themselves coaches, are falling into the trap of trying to rescue, save or heal their clients. They view their clients as broken and in need of rehabilitation in some way. This is the exact opposite of what I believe coaching to be, where two people, the coach and the client enter the relationship in an equal, "I'm ok, you're ok" mindset. Coaching sessions may have a therapeutic feel to them, in the same way that walking, reading or fishing may do, but it isn't therapy.

Coaching isn't Teaching

Teaching is about the transfer of knowledge or skills from a teacher to a student. The teacher knows something, and they attempt, by a variety of means, to teach the student what it is they know, so that the student can share in that knowledge or skill. Most of what has traditionally been called sports coaching, is in fact teaching, not coaching at all. The sports coach knows how the game should be played or the techniques involved, and they teach the athletes this knowledge. Sir John Whitmore, one of the founding fathers of modern day coaching, makes the point, *"For some reason we have tennis coaches but ski instructors. Both for the most part, in my experience, are instructors."* Both are much more like teachers than coaches. In coaching there is no aim for the transfer of knowledge or skills. I believe the coaching role becomes more like coaching and less like teaching at the top end of professional sport. As elite athletes have a great grasp of the basic techniques and perhaps need help to simply figure out for themselves how they can make marginal gains, rather than being taught new skills. In true coaching, the coach is not attempting to teach the client anything. Although transfer of knowledge may occur by default, as it always does in any relationship, it is not the primary aim. The coach trusts that the client already has all they need and empowers them to tap into and use their current knowledge and skills.

Coaching isn't a Programme

Coaching is often associated with some kind of personal development programme, or business growth accelerator course, where participants are walked through a series of prescribed activities, from stage to stage, in order to grow themselves or their business. Although, when this is done well, there can be great merit in this type of course, it isn't coaching. A programme like this may use a coaching style or a coaching approach but it isn't coaching. Coaching is not something that is done *to* people and coaching does not have a prescribed path, or a step-by-step guide attached to it. The true essence of coaching is only found in an open space, where the client has the freedom to walk their own path, at their own pace with a coach working alongside them empowering them to make new discoveries, see fresh options and move forward in their own way.

Coaching isn't Motivational Speaking

Many motivational speakers also carry the title coach. I, myself, do some speaking, but when I'm speaking, I'm not coaching. They are two very different things. Speaking is much more like a modern form of preaching, where people are simply stating their thoughts and beliefs, with a view to helping people think differently. Again, if it's done well, it can be incredible, but it isn't coaching. Coaching isn't about the coach stating their thoughts or beliefs in order to help the client change, it's about understanding and exploring the client's beliefs, in order to help them grow themselves.

What Coaching Is

There are plenty of ideas and definitions of what coaching is in a plethora of books on the subject. Judith Tolhurst says, *"Coaching is a way of working alongside someone, giving him/her the opportunity to set goals and the support to achieve them."* Julie Starr defines coaching in this way, *"Coaching is a conversation, or series of conversations, that one person has with another. The person who is the coach intends to produce a conversation that will benefit the other person (the coachee) in a way that relates to the coachee's learning and progress."* The creators of the Co-Active Coaching Model write, *"We believe that coaching is chiefly about discovery, awareness and choice. It is a way of effectively empowering people to find their own answers, encouraging and supporting them on the path as they continue to make important life-giving and life-changing choices."*

Beyond nit-picking, there is nothing within any of these explanations of coaching which I fundamentally disagree with and all of them provide us with some insight into the nature of coaching. I would never claim to have the definitive definition. When I set about trying to define coaching, it became apparent that to take something as beautifully complex as coaching, with all the wonder it creates and feelings it evokes and place it into a sentence would not do it justice, no matter how intricate or clever my use of words.

Putting coaching into a one or two sentence definition, is like trying to take the vastness of the ocean and pour it into a tin can or take the wonders of the night sky and squeeze them it into a shoe-box. Coaching will spill over the limitations of any words used to describe it, because it is so much greater than the boundaries of our language and ultimately it is something which must be experienced to be fully understood.

All I can do therefore, is say to the best of my ability what coaching has become for me. My current understanding of coaching is not my final version. What it is for me at this moment, is quite different from how I would have defined it at the beginning of my coaching journey. If I am to continue to grow as a person and as a coach, then my understanding of coaching will evolve with me. My limited definition of coaching currently reads in this way, *"Coaching is a partnership that empowers people to take ownership for their own development."*

There are four key words in this definition which are worth noting:

Partnership means there must be an equality within the coaching relationship, without any sense of hierarchy. A true partnership between coach and client that offers mutual respect and creates a connection where both partners contribute in their own unique way.

Empowers is not about the coach giving power to the client, as though the coach has all the power and hands it over to the client. There is no transfer of power with coaching, because empowerment truly happens when a client discovers or unlocks the power that already exists within them and a coach partners with them in that journey.

Ownership is about the client taking responsibility for their own thoughts, decisions, perspectives and actions. Coaching empowers a client to take ownership of their life and circumstances, whilst also enabling them to recognise what they do and don't have ownership over.

Development must be both an internal and external process and coaching is always about the growth of the client in some way. This may be progress in the way they feel or see the world, or how they behave and the actions they take.

As coaching starts to emerge out of the shadow and confusion of other disciplines and sits more prominently in its own light, I hope we can begin to grasp what sets it apart as a way of working and communicating with people. Yet, we must now enter the most challenging and sacred part of coaching. It is the place that most people stumble in their coaching development and the area in which some self-proclaimed coaches do not dare to tread. Yet to truly see the power and magic of coaching we must learn to embrace the land of the unknowing.

Chapter 2

Unknowing - Into the Great Unknown

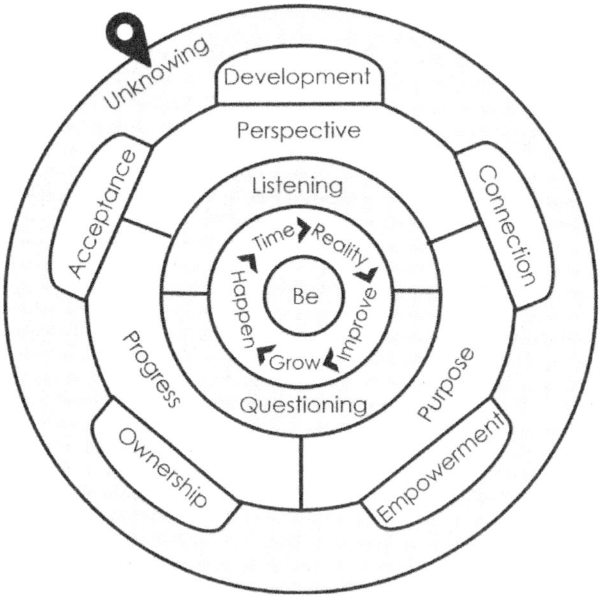

"Some people long for a life that is simple and planned

Tied with a ribbon

Some people won't sail the sea 'cause they're safer on land

To follow what's written

But I'd follow you to the great unknown

Off to a world we call our own."

Michelle Williams, Tightrope, The Greatest Showman

Knowing

"If you don't know this, you shouldn't be here" roared my maths teacher. Sitting in class, staring at the blackboard, not knowing the answer to the question he was posing was excruciating. I grew up in a district where at the age of 11, at the end of our primary education, all the kids sat a test to see whether we would go to the local high school or the grammar school. I went to a tiny primary school, which was so small that a few years previous it had been on the verge of closure. There were only two classrooms in the whole school, one for the infants and one for the juniors. There were just four other children my age and when we first moved to the area, my brother's attendance doubled the numbers in his year group. It was a wonderful place to go to school. The toilets might have been outside, and we never had a proper football pitch, but the attention and love we got in that place was amazing. Everyone knew everyone else, and thinking back, even though I was top of my year for most subjects, the teachers there were interested in us as individuals, not just our academic ability. At grammar school it was a very different story. When I arrived there, not only did I discover that my academic ability placed me somewhere more in the middle of the pack, but it felt like my whole value was no longer placed on who I was, but rather on what I did and didn't know.

Some people held being at grammar school in great esteem, like it in some way made us elite. I, on the other hand, found that whole attitude irritating because from a young age I've been disinterested in people's status or titles. Some of my teachers were fantastic, but there was this soul destroying, reoccurring phrase I heard from a few of the teaching staff on a regular basis. The first time it was spoken, I was just two days into my time at my new school. I recall it vividly. In a maths lesson, the teacher was explaining a concept and posing us a question, and I just didn't understand it. I was quite good at maths and didn't struggle too much with many of the theories, but in this moment as he was asking us to write the answer in our books, I just didn't know. I wasn't the only one, because looking around there were several bewildered faces. After a few moments of puzzlement, on the other side of the class room, Jill, a quiet girl with mousey hair and big bottle-rimmed glasses, put her hand up and admitted, *"Sir, I don't know the answer!"* Out of my teacher's mouth came the phrase I was to hear repeatedly over the years and it still conjures feelings of agitation within me. *"If you don't know this, you shouldn't be here,"* came his response. He, along with the other teachers I heard the same phrase from over the years, were communicating to us that if we didn't know, we weren't good enough and that only in having knowledge were we of worth. From that very young age, I learnt to dread not knowing and fear the great unknown. At my school, it seemed I was only of worth when I did know. My education system taught me that *not knowing* was more than just a bad thing, it was shameful. The old mantra of 'knowledge is power' was an absolute truth in that place. On reflection I can see how this shaped my early life. I would dodge situations of uncertainty and avoid the unknown at all costs. It led me to only ever attempt tasks that I knew I could achieve and swerve anything that placed me into a state of unknowing.

Unknowing is Power

Sometimes knowledge is power, except when it isn't; because sometimes knowledge is the opposite of power, sometimes it actually cripples all the power that exists. It is often the unknown where the power truly lies and the unknown that brings the spark to a situation. As good as knowledge is, at times, it also has the power to kill possibilities. When we are utterly certain about something, it restricts the opportunities and options for anything else to exist. Knowing hems people in and narrows their path, whereas not-knowing widens the road ahead, like an ocean opening up from the river mouth. It is in the unknown that people begin to explore and discover. There is nothing wrong with gathering knowledge, in fact doing so can often develop and grow us, upskill us and empower us. However, the problem lies more with our struggle to handle our sense of not-knowing. I witness adults finding moments of unknowing excruciating. Yet, the unknown is exactly where we need to be in our quest to help people grow themselves.

I was taught the story as a child that when Christopher Columbus sailed across the Atlantic to discover the Americas, he was scared he would sail right off the edge of the earth, and that his voyage finally dispelled the theory of a Flat Earth. Although I now know this version of events to be untrue, it does display to us the restricting power of knowing, or at least thinking we know. There was a time when many civilisations 'knew' the world was flat and if you were to venture too far from land you may well drop right off, so no-one travelled that way because everybody knew it was risky. It was only once people started to doubt this knowing and enter into a state of unknowing that they were able to explore and discover. Knowing isn't always as powerful as not-knowing, because it is the unknown that creates our desire to search, to explore and seek endless possibilities for growth.

I don't want a Doctor who doesn't know, I don't want a Police Detective who doesn't know, and I don't even want a Weather Forecaster who doesn't know. It's their job to know, they get paid to know and when I need to call upon their services, I want them to know. However, it's my job as a coach to not know and as soon as I start thinking I do know, I've stopped doing the job people are paying me for.

Therefore, I spend most of my working life (and a lot of the rest of my life) in a state of not knowing and what a beautiful place it is to be. In my unknowing, comes all the power and possibility for others and myself to grow. "I don't know" has become my most useful of all mindsets and I am now pleased to be a coach who doesn't know.

It can be difficult to cope with not-knowing something. Our culture seems to revere knowledge and despise the unknown. Often not-knowing is seen as a weakness, or a vulnerability that must be covered over and never revealed. Yet, all we so often do with our knowledge, is kill the art of exploration and discovery. We are so sure we know something, that any other possibility is dismissed. Eckhart Tolle in his thought-provoking book, *A New Earth* puts it wonderfully when he writes, *"Everything, a bird, a tree, even a simple stone, and certainly a human being, is ultimately unknowable. This is because it has unfathomable depth".*

I wonder how often our sense of knowing limits and hinders our potential for discovery. Yet once we are able to accept the unknowable, then perhaps we are also able to plunge to greater depths. Which is why I urge all coaches to create a mindset that embraces the unknown, because without it we will never serve our clients as fully as we ought.

Non-Directive

Coaching at its most powerful is a non-directive process. This means it is not the coach who is the expert or leader of the session, but rather it is the client who is the decision maker, vision giver and pace-setter. Carl Rogers the creator of the person-centred model developed the idea of non-directive work in the 1940's and 1950's and Mark Prever tells us it was "*largely as a reaction to the analytical approaches that predominated at the time.*" In a coaching sense non-directive work simply means empowering the client to find their own way forward with no advice, direction or judgement coming from the coach. Directive work, on the other hand, is when a coach decides they have the answer for their client and sets the direction a client will take by either telling, hinting or persuading a client down a certain path. In coaching, the coach is never the expert or guru for the client. In fact, because a client has come to coaching to talk about themselves, it is they that hold the expertise on the subject matter. They are the only person in the world who has ever lived and experienced their life, therefore they know the subject matter far better than any coach ever could. It is the coach's job to be in a state of unknowing. Not knowing what is best for the client, not knowing the way forward and not knowing what any of the answers for them are.

I love Rogers' bravery and vision to step away from the cultural ideas that surrounded him, of the practitioner being the expert who would analyse and prescribe for their clients and instead, place the client firmly as the expert in the room. Despite it being generations since Rogers' theories first emerged, the idea of a person being the expert on themselves, seems to be the exact opposite of what we continue to find in our day to day lives. Most individuals still believe that what others need above anything else is advice, and if they have listened to somebody's story for two or three minutes, then they have all the answers and solutions that person could ever need. Nancy Kline writes it wonderfully as she describes what happens to most of us when a friend calls with a problem, *"You assume the caller's brain, the one that contained the problem, did not also contain the solution. You assumed because you had been taught this almost since you could breathe, that helping people means thinking for them. The thing you do, therefore, would be to listen only as long as it took your brain to think of an idea for them. Then you would say it, expect them to see the genius in it and be grateful."*

When my wife and I were going through the process of adopting a child, it was fascinating to hear people giving advice about what we should and shouldn't do; or how we should or shouldn't approach something. They were just so certain they knew what was right for us. Advice was presented such as "*You really need to think about the impact on your biological children*" or *"It'll probably be alright when he's little, but have you thought about his teenage years"* and even *"He'll have attachment issues because I've watched a documentary about it on the TV"*. I occasionally asked these advice-givers how long they had been thinking about the issue of our adoption. "*Well, just since you started talking about it a few minutes ago",* was the most common response. In contrast, my wife and I had been thinking about adoption for over a decade. Ten or more years of talking, thinking, wrestling, challenging and 'to and froing' over what this might mean for us and our children. Yet people who had been considering it for less than five minutes, felt they knew and had some pearls of wisdom we hadn't thought of. It's ridiculous when you think of it in these terms. It is the same for our clients, whether they are talking about a problem or a goal, it is certain they have spent more time working with the topic, than the coach has spent listening to it. Our job as a coach, is not to solve our clients' problems for them or tell them exactly how to achieve their goals, but rather to empower them to tap into the expertise which already exists within them. Provide them with the space to figure it out for themselves, to find their own way forward. Only in embracing the unknowing and recognising that we don't know what is best for our clients can we truly learn to be non-directive.

It is vital as a coach we strive to continually hold a non-directive approach in our work with our clients. I'm not suggesting that within coaching it is possible, nor appropriate, to be 100% non-directive in every single moment with our clients, as it perhaps is within some other practices. None-the-less, the unknowing and non-directiveness must be a starting point and an ongoing aim for all coaches to consistently strive after, and any decision to veer from that path must be done with good reason and in the best interests of our client. To remain fully non-directive at all times, would perhaps lead the coach to a place of complete passivity, where they did nothing at all. I am aware that as soon as I open my mouth, I am in some small way becoming directive. By choosing to ask one question over another, I am in some way allowing a degree of directiveness into the session. Therefore, I am not overly concerned with debates over where exactly non-directiveness becomes directiveness. Rather, the importance is in coaches being able to resist any temptation to be the expert or advice-giver in the room and empower their clients to trust themselves to find their own path. Carl Rogers put in perfectly when he said, *"it began to occur to me that unless I had a need to demonstrate my own cleverness and learning, I would do better to rely upon the client for the direction of movement in the process."*

Maps of the World

The reason non-directive work brings so much more potential for growth than directive work is because non-directive coaching enables people to make paradigm shifts. Changes in the way they see the world that allow them to move forward in different, more helpful ways. Carl Rogers describes people's paradigms as their *"frame of reference"* and I love the way that Stephen Covey in The 7 Habits of Highly Effective People refers to people's paradigms as their *"map of their world".* It conjures up an image of each of us wandering around with an invisible map of our world, held out in front of us. On that map is all the information we need to make sense of the world we live in. This imagery shows us how and why people are seeing and experiencing the world the way they do. For each of us, our map represents the way in which the world is for us and we use our maps to check and interpret our world in a way that enables us to make sense of our experiences. We filter every word, interaction, circumstance or observation through our maps and we do all this without even consciously thinking about it. If we accept the idea that everyone holds an invisible map of their world, we can start to understand the difficulties we often face, within our communication with each other. The problem starts with everybody's map being completely unique. Each map has been built since the beginning of our lives through our own individual experiences, upbringing, culture and interpretations of our world. Nobody has ever lived the life you have, experienced what you have experienced and made sense of it the way you do. Even siblings raised in the same family will have unique maps of their world. This means our maps don't immediately make any sense to each other and our worlds can often collide. It's as though our maps are written in different languages from one another's. It's easy to see the difference in our maps simply by asking a group of people to check their own map around the very same word. For example, if I was to ask ten people in the same room what the word "family" means for them, they would all instantly check their own map and without doubt, I would receive ten different interpretations of that same word. Perhaps for one person "family" will mean a very safe and supportive place, for another a dysfunctional, difficult environment, for another loving, yet strained relationships. One word as simple as *family*, is interpreted in utterly unique ways by each individual person because each person's map of the world tells them something different. If, therefore, our client begins to talk about their family, it is our job as a coach to really try to understand what *they* mean by family, not assume we know and understand because we are interpreting *family* through our own map. What their map says about family and what our map says, will almost certainly be different in some way. If we think we know and are listening and asking questions based on our own map we will consistently misinterpret what it is our client truly means.

The big flaw in being directive, is that advice always comes off our own map, it comes from the way in which we see the world and not the way in which our client sees the world. We may have experienced a very similar situation and our client may even be talking about aspects that ring true for us in our own story. However, even two remarkably similar experiences will still be vastly different because of the way in which those experiences have been individually interpreted.

I'm not against all advice, some advice is good, some advice is wise, and some advice is clever; yet advice can never be as powerful as allowing someone the opportunity to figure something out for themselves, to find their own solutions and make their own way forward. As Nancy Kline continues, *"Your ideas are not their ideas. And so they were not quite as good – not quite as accurate, as rich, as just right as theirs would have been."* As I have worked in an unknowing way and through a non-directive basis, allowing my clients to figure it out, time after time I have been blown away with the fact that the ideas they create, are almost always far better than any suggestions I may have had for them. It is simply because, when they are given the time and space to think through whatever it might be, their expertise and understanding of themselves permits them to find their perfect solution. Any advice I might have for them, would only be based within my own experience of my world and not rooted in their world, therefore it is always polluted, always flawed and not as helpful as the advice they can find within themselves.

Inappropriately Non-Directive

There are some circumstances in life which do require a very directive approach with people, where they simply need to be told what to do and when to do it. If, for example, in the middle of the night a fire alarm sounds in a house where a family are sleeping, it would be ridiculous for the parents to remain non-directive with their children, asking them, "how do you feel about the smoke? or "what would you like to do next?" It is a life-threatening situation and requires a very directive response. The parents would very quickly, in that instance, give their children precise instructions on what they need to do, or if possible, scoop their children up from bed and carry them out of the house themselves. There are clearly circumstances in life which do call for us to be directive with people.

It can also be unhelpful to work on a non-directive basis with someone where there is a clear knowledge gap about important information or facts. If a client has a hole in their map of the world, where there is no information within themselves about that particular subject because they simply don't know a fact, a non-directive approach can prove frustrating. I know next-to-nothing about car engines and if I found myself in a position where there was something wrong with my car engine and I needed to make an attempt at fixing it, the last thing I would want is someone working on a non-directive basis with me. Particularly if they held the information that I needed. It would prove infuriating to me to have a non-directive mechanic stood next to me as I opened the car bonnet asking me questions, such as "What would be the most helpful thing you could do next?" or "What does the sound the engine is making mean to you?" I just wouldn't know. I have a knowledge gap about the workings of a car engine and I would need some information about that subject before I could hope to be engaged in a non-directive conversation. It's important to recognise there is a huge difference between giving advice and sharing some knowledge. Advice is telling people what you think they should do, whereas sharing knowledge is the passing on of information about a certain fact or topic. On very rare occasions, it may be useful for a coach to share some knowledge about facts, but hardly ever useful for them to give advice.

Going Directive

Even when it is perfectly viable, a non-directive approach can be overlooked in favour of a directive approach for a number of reasons. We can be tempted to use a directive approach simply because it is quicker. As coaches, we can become so focussed on our client "getting there" rather than the process or journey that is taking place for them, we will jump to telling them how they should get there rather than empowering them to discover for themselves. Non-directive work will often take longer to arrive at a solution or goal, because the client is working out their own way forward. However, when they do figure it out for themselves it creates in them much longer-lasting growth than if they are acting upon the instructions of someone else. If a client is told to do something, there remains a high possibility they won't truly commit to it, won't do it. Even if they do, they certainly won't take ownership for their development. Directive work can and does have some impact, but on most occasions it only creates short-term changes in people. When once again left to their own devices they will more than likely return to their previous ways. If a client makes their own choices and decisions about what they are going to do, then they probably will follow through on those choices, take full responsibility for their own development and create within themselves a permanence of growth that will outlive the coaching relationship.

We can also take a directive approach because we want to help our client and have decided we know what is best for them. Our desire to use a directive approach often comes from a place of good intention, in that we genuinely want to help them. Yet in our belief we are giving something useful to them, we don't recognise what we are taking in the same breath. We might hand a person a solution to their problem, but in doing so we often rob them of the learning, the exploration and the discovering of the exact right answer for themselves. In working on a directive basis with people, we disempower them and create a relationship of reliance, where they become dependent on us for all the ideas and solutions.

Often when people first come across the idea of working in the unknown and on a non-directive basis with people, they can fall into the trap of *pseudo non-directiveness*. They buy into the concept of non-directiveness and so attempt to outwardly appear to be not advising or directing in any way and yet inwardly, they have fallen into old habits of quickly deciding exactly what they think their client should or shouldn't do. What then occurs is the coach dropping hints, or asking loaded questions, in a way that pushes or manipulates a client down a certain path towards what the coach has decided is the right course of action. To be truly non-directive means to start from a place of not-knowing and embrace the unknowing part of you. Not having the answers for your client and learning to trust that that they know best is the greatest gift you can offer them.

Living a Coaching Approach

Although, for the most part, coaching will take place through a series of focused conversations in a private room between a qualified coach and a client. There is also space for a 'coaching approach' to penetrate the whole of our lives in the way we interact with others. Coaching has been happening in much less prescribed ways throughout the history of humanity. It might not have been called coaching, but it was still taking place. It is possible for us to adopt a 'coaching approach' attitude to life, an ability to begin from a non-directive, unknowing place which infiltrates almost all interactions we have with others. This coaching approach to life starts to flow by learning to trust that people are capable, they can find their own answers even when they perhaps seem like they can't, they can figure it out and they don't need us to do it for them. This also means we must learn to offer this same trust to ourselves, to know that we are also capable. Susan Jeffers in her infamous book 'Feel the Fear and Do It Anyway' tells us, "*What matters is that you begin now to develop trust in yourself, until you reach the point where you will be able to say. Whatever happens to me, given any situation, I can handle it.*" Imagine what life might be like if we were able to trust our own and other people's ability to handle it, no matter what it was. Imagine if we could adopt this 'coaching approach' to life where it simply wasn't our job to solve other people's problems or tell them what they should do, but rather to empower them and to trust them to handle it. What often happens in our relationships, parenting and work places, is a reliance on being told what to do and culture of dependency where people are disempowered from creating their own way of doing things. Imagine a world where parents empower their children, managers empower their staff and spouses empower one another by trusting the resilience, creativity and drive that lies within each of us to develop and grow. I'm not suggesting for a moment we can parent our children in a completely non-directive way, nor do I believe that as a manager we could give our staff complete free-reign. I do however, whole-heartedly believe we would witness greater growth in the people around us, if we were able to embrace a coaching approach to life.

The Not-Knowing Coach

When I work on a non-directive basis with people it drives me into a place of unknowing. Not knowing what is best, not knowing where the conversation is going, not knowing if it will be helpful for the client and not even knowing what my next question might be. In order to work this way, I have to have an unrelenting trust in humans to find their own way forward. I also must have trust in myself, trust in my relationship with my client and trust in the coaching process. I know that this works. I've seen it play out time and time again and yet I also know in the early stages of working this way, I struggled to hold this level of trust in all these elements. Mainly, because I wanted to be good at coaching, I wanted to get it right and I wanted to feel helpful to my client. Yet I've discovered all this just gets in the way of quality coaching. At first it sounds strange to hear this, but to truly be good at coaching we must rid ourselves of any desire to be good or to be getting it right. It isn't about getting it right, because while we are thinking about being good at it, we aren't really being with our client and being with our client is the most important part. We must learn to make peace with the unknowing. All it takes to do so, is to let go of being in control and trust the person in front of us. On our coaching training courses, one of the most common themes in practice coaching sessions is that the novice coach feels 'stuck'. They are unsure what to ask next, or how best to empower their client. What is lacking in this moment, is not so much a deficiency in skill, but rather a lack of trust in themselves to risk 'not getting it right'. As I witness coaches really beginning to have faith in themselves, their client and the coaching process, this sense of being stuck begins to happen far less frequently. They begin to realise there is very little scope in coaching for being right or being wrong, there is only the sense of being with another person and in that moment trusting the client to find their own path.

Put Our Maps Away

We must be able to take our own map of our world, fold it up and keep it under our chair for the duration of a coaching session. We must discipline ourselves to focus entirely on our client's map and to do everything in our power to see the world through their eyes. It will take some time to master this way of working. We are so used to instinctively checking our own map, that to put it away for a time can be very difficult and often, particularly early on in our coaching training, we may find our map getting involved in the coaching session. We must discipline ourselves to keep putting it away, each and every time we find ourselves filtering our client's words through our own map and move our focus back to their world. As we continue to do this, it becomes easier and easier to keep our own map out of the coaching room. It may take some time to learn to trust this process and trust our client's expertise, but it is vital we do, because it is in the unknowing where the real power of coaching lays.

Chapter 3

Development - Growing or Changing?

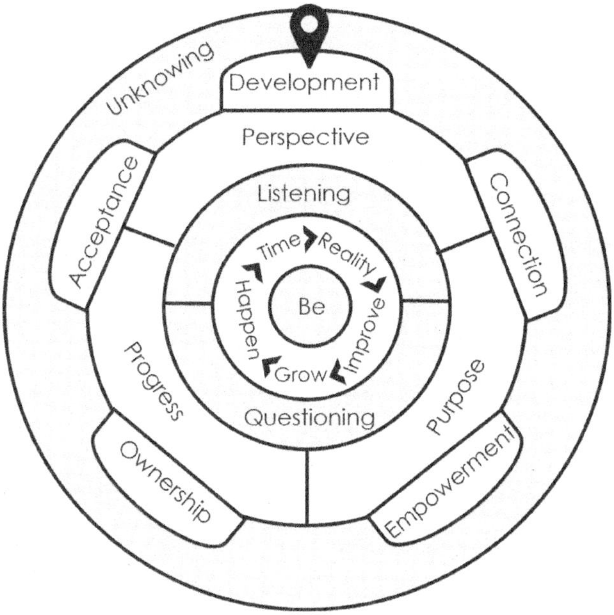

"Change may not always bring growth, but there is no growth without change."

Roy T. Bennett, The Light in the Heart

Big Change

The 1988 movie *Big* paints us a wonderful and hilarious story of change; where a 12-year-old boy called Josh, experiences the most dramatic of all transformations. One evening when a fair comes to town Josh finds himself turned away from one of the attractions, because he isn't tall enough to ride it. Even more frustratingly for Josh, his rejection from the ride takes place in full view of the good-looking girl he is trying desperately to impress. Embarrassed and angry, he flees deeper into the fair, until breathless, he stumbles upon Zoltan, the mysterious genie machine. Drawn to the bizarre humanoid puppet within the glass casing, Josh puts his money in the slot and makes a simple wish to be taller, to be bigger. Obviously, nothing happens, so he wanders home dejected and down trodden. Yet, he awakes the next morning to discover his wish granted. Not only is Josh bigger, he has transformed overnight into the body of a 30-year-old man. His clothes don't fit, his voice has broken, and his mum clearly doesn't recognise him. She screams in horror at the sight of this strange grown up in her house. In utter panic Josh struggles to know what to do or where to go. He realises his only hope is to find his best friend, Billy. It takes a concerted effort, but eventually Josh is able to convince Billy, that this man before him is in fact his 12-year-old friend. Realising he can't go home, the two friends figure out a way to set Josh up in a New York apartment with a job at a toy company, where he not only wins the favour of his boss but also begins a relationship with one of his female colleagues. On the outside Josh starts to look like a proper adult, he has a home, a relationship and a successful job, but on the inside, he still feels and thinks like a 12 year-old kid. He was changed from 12 to 30 years old overnight and even though it appears as if Josh has grown,. he hasn't really, he has just simply changed.

The Difference

We often confuse changing with growing. We cannot grow without changing, but we can most certainly change without growing. This is where the confusion lies. Josh changed quickly and dramatically, but, other than physically, he didn't grow. He skipped the growing process and therefore couldn't handle the change when it arrived and longed to return to his 12-year-old state. We often believe if we make a change, we have grown and yet this is rarely the case. We can change in all sorts of ways without moving a single inch forward. We can change without ever developing ourselves in any way whatsoever, and people often do. We can change a relationship by ending one and starting another, it doesn't mean we have grown, we can change jobs or get a promotion, it doesn't mean any growing has taken place. We can change our appearance in all sorts of ways, yet it doesn't mean we have grown at all. As people and as coaches we mustn't confuse change with growth, because if we do, we run the risk of coaching our clients to change rather than grow. We could celebrate change when there has been no real growth and we could miss the growing our clients have done because we are so busy looking for change. Our focus as coaches must be upon our clients' growth and development, not on their change. We are all capable of making changes, whereas growing is a whole lot trickier.

Changing is often not even a choice. Changing is inevitable and unrelenting for all of us. Whether we want to or not, we are changing. Everything around us is changing too, it always has, and it always will. We humans live in an ever-changing world, an ever-changing body, an ever-changing mind and an ever-changing set of circumstances. We can attempt, as many do, to try and slow the process of change, to put the brakes on, but we can never stop it. Nothing is as it once was, no matter how hard we try to keep it that way. There is no standing still in the human world, however much we would love there to be. The passing of time ensures life itself is an ever-changing ocean of ebb and flow. The question for us is not whether we want to change, but rather whether we want to grow? Are we prepared to embrace our development, take charge of it and chart our own course?

Carl Rogers famously noted that all living things (from potatoes to human beings) have an inclination towards growth. In essence, it is in our very nature to develop and progress. It is something he referred to as the 'actualising tendency' and I whole-heartedly buy into his theories on this. I believe we were born to grow and develop, to move forward and make progress. It is our natural state of being. Yet this tendency is tarnished as we progress through our upbringing and our adult lives, by our cultures, societies, care-givers and a whole host of other factors. Rogers believed our innate desire to grow is stunted or warped by our conditioning. Therefore, as much as change is often not a choice, growing most certainly is. How we grow is something we must consciously choose to create, something we must tap into and make happen for ourselves, otherwise the pressures of this world will stop that development in its tracks.

Growing is Scary

Stephen Grosz, in his beautiful book The Examined Life said *"We feel unable to go forward and yet believe that there must be a way. 'I want to change, but not if change means changing' a patient once said to me in complete innocence."* This is even truer for growth, with the reality for so many of us that we love and hate growing in equal measure. We chase after it and then hide from it, we long for it but fear it, we hope it will happen but wish for things to remain the same. Growing is scary. It's also divisive because so much of us wants to grow, to develop and improve ourselves in whatever way that might be, yet another part of us is frightened to walk the path into the unknown and find out what that means for us.

About 4000 years ago, Moses led the nation of Israel out of slavery in Egypt. He freed them from generations of subjugation and the brutally of their Egyptian masters and took them out across the desert towards the promised land. Yet, despite all this, despite perhaps longing for their liberty for so long, some of the Israelites still weren't happy. Rather than thanking Moses and praising him for his efforts in prizing them out of the grip of oppression, they grumbled and complained at him, asking him to take them back to Egypt. They didn't like the desert, it was different, difficult and harsh. Coupled with that, they didn't know what the promised land looked like or what it might mean for them. They told Moses to return them to Egypt, to slavery. They wanted to go back. Back to the dominion and rule of Egypt because even though they were slaves, without very much of a life at all, they knew what that life looked like. They knew what to expect and how that world moved. Egypt wasn't as scary for them as the desert or the promised land, because even though it was hard, they understood the rules in Egypt. They knew what life would be like, they had a clear vision of their existence in Egypt. They longed for this certainty more than they longed for their freedom and the chance to build a new, yet unknown life. I'm sure there was division in the Israelites, not just amongst them as a group, but inside them as individuals. Part of them longing for growth, for freedom and yet another part so scared of the unknown they would rather choose not to grow at all.

After spending virtually my entire adult life in the business of helping individuals develop, I believe this is not just the story of the Israelites but the story of all humans. We want to grow, to move forward, to improve but we also don't want to, because even when the growth looks positive, our fear of the unknown forces us to try and return to what we know.

The Totality of Growth

Grosz tells us *"there cannot be change without loss,"* and there most certainly cannot be growth without loss, because growing contains both gains and losses. There can be no gain without simultaneous loss. We cannot make a gain in our life without shedding something at the same time. Gain and loss co-exist in our lives like conjoined twins. Where one is, there the other will also be. I used to see gain as a positive word and loss as a negative word, yet now I see they both have the potential to be either. On occasions, the greatest growth we can create is firstly about losing something. At times, loss can be incredibly positive for us. The two go hand in hand and the more we gain, the more we lose, the less we lose the less we gain. In order to grow in life, we must on occasions, lose friends, lose jobs, lose comfort, lose money, lose sleep and a whole host of other things as well. In order to lose in life, we must sometimes gain courage, gain certainty, gain relationships, gain respect, gain new perspectives and a multitude of others.

Growing is a holistic process that traverses the full range of gain and loss and we fear gain and loss in equal measure; which is why as coaches we must be acutely aware of the whole process of growth within our clients. I often witness a strong emphasis in coaching on what people are gaining from it, without the same attention being applied to what people are losing. To work with the whole person, we must see that growing encompasses both gain and loss simultaneously, in equal measure and brings with it equal trepidation. The real fear is not so much about the gain and loss, but more so about the unknown. I have come to believe humanity's greatest fear is simply the unknown and the greatest unknown we experience is our future. We know the past, we experienced it, we know the present because we are living it, but what none of us truly know is the future. We like to think we do because we create what Grosz refers to as a "*predicted future*". We anticipate our future and it brings us some comfort to believe we know how things are going to play out. However, we only know this if everything stays more or less the same as it is now. If we begin the process of growing, our predicted futures become uncertain and unclear. In order to grow we have to look into the great unknown and in that process what we truly lose is our predicted futures and our sense of knowing how things will be. This is the reason, even when we are ready to grow, we can experience conflict inside ourselves, because to let go of our "predicted future" and embrace instead an "unknown future" is a frightening concept for us. As coaches we must be aware and always listening for the totality of the growing process for our clients, with all their gains and losses. If we become too focused upon only what our clients will gain, we create the danger of them inadvertently losing something of great importance to them.

Growing is a Journey

Growth is a process and it has to be this way, yet I see people chasing after instant progress, over-night success and immediate results, almost on a daily basis. There are hundreds of fad diets that claim vast amounts of weight loss within days, self-help gurus who testify to having completely changed a person's life in seven minutes of conversation and too many get-rich-quick schemes to mention. People seem to be looking for some magic wand, or genie in a bottle who will grant them all the development and change they desire in an instance. There is no magic wand, no genie in a bottle. It's a blessing for us all, because if there was and we did have access to instantaneous growth, we wouldn't be able to cope with it. We need the journey of growing even more than we need the destination. In *Big,* young Josh skipped the journey of growth, which meant he couldn't cope with the destination when it arrived, he yearned to return to his 12-year-old self, to go back to what he knew. The growth had come too quickly, and he had missed the process.

Humans need the process. Growth that happens too quickly in my experience only creates a short-term result. Without the journey and process of development there is no permanence to it. I have very little interest in short-term growth because we are all capable of this. Growth in the short-term is easy. We can all begin a new diet, modify our outward behaviour or create a New Year's resolution for a while. It doesn't last though, because we are skipping the journey. We are trying to jump from 12 years old to 30 years old overnight, we are trying to teleport ourselves from Egypt to the Promised Land and bypass the desert. In order to create long-term growth in ourselves and others, we must embrace the journey, as difficult as it may be. There is no short cut, despite what many would claim.

As coaches it is vital we embrace the process and journey of development within our clients. To rush this process for them is to undo all the great work taking place. There is nothing worse than an impatient coach who wants the client's growth more than the client themselves. It is a law of nature that we must take into the coaching relationship. Nature doesn't rush its growth, it hugs the journey and lets it unfold. Rushing the process creates fear in our clients and in many ways stunts the growth that is taking place. Parents who pressure their children to grow up too quickly and farmers who pick fruit before it is ripe both stunt the process of growth in their own way. As coaches we must be conscious of the growth of our client, but never ever demanding of a timescale. People will grow, at the right pace and in the right time for them, if we provide a safe, helpful environment in which to do so.

Real Growth is Inside Out

Real growth in humans happens on the inside first. It works from inside to out, not from the outside to in. People often attempt to create growth by changing their outside circumstances, whilst ignoring their inner world. We can get a new hair-cut, lose some weight, end a relationship, start a new job or move to a new house. However, if this change doesn't come from an internal growth in the way we think or feel towards that particular circumstance then the outside change will only ever be temporary. At some point the outside change will run out of steam, it will dry up and we will return to our old patterns.

Real growth comes from the inside, not from the outside. We can change our outside all we want but if the inside never develops then no real, permanent result has taken place. We must learn to consciously understand our inner thoughts and feelings, that drive our choices and actions on the outside, only then can we grow in the direction we want to.

We also must accept we cannot force real growth on anyone else. Real growth is something that only happens through conscious choice. It must come from the person themselves, it can't be done to people and can't be done for people. Real growth takes ownership, awareness and intention. Many people promise transformation and claim they can empower others to grow by following this plan or that programme, but I cannot create growth in or for anyone else. I can only create the best setting and environment for them, to give them the best chance of working it out for themselves. It has to come from them, from the inside of them otherwise it is a wholly pointless activity. I trust wholeheartedly in people's capacity to figure out their own development. Real growth therefore can never be forced, it cannot be faked, and it can't be done *to* anyone.

Unless we are able to grow our internal world, we will never truly be able to develop. Our world view creates within us a default setting, where no matter how much we try and grow on the outside we will continually spring back to the default setting of our world view. As a child, one of my favourite toys was Stretch Armstrong because I loved pulling and wrenching it as far as it would go in to all kinds of weird shapes. Stretch Armstrong was a simple child's toy, a muscular action figure with blonde hair and skimpy speedos. It was only a few inches tall but so elasticated it could be stretched out for what, as a child, seemed like miles. The real beauty of a Stretch Armstrong was not so much its stretchiness, but in its ability to always spring back to its original size, its default setting. It could consistently change temporarily, without ever growing permanently. It reminds me so much of people and how our dominant world view causes us to spring back. Often, what we refer to as 'change' within coaching is only really helping people to change on the outside without ever really growing on the inside. Enabling people to change in the short-term, without ever truly growing in the long-term. New Year Resolutions hint at the idea that we all have it within us to make a change and they are also the best example we see where, for most people, growth doesn't last. There is no permanence to these New Year Resolutions. They are purely external changes, they are people attempting to change their actions or the way in which they behave. Yet, our behaviours and actions are only ever a clue to what is going on under the surface for us, they are simply the way in which our inner self manifests itself on the outside. Therefore, any attempt to change the outer self without first developing our inner world, will only ever be a temporary result, a scaffolding which holds our actions and behaviours in place for however long the scaffolding stands up. As soon as the scaffolding is removed the behaviours return to their default setting. We spring back like a Stretch Armstrong being released from the hands of a child. Our drive towards changed behaviours can in fact look impressive but are often nothing more than a temporary external change. As a coach, I am far more interested in the internal growth of my clients than anything they do on the outside, because I know when people develop on the inside the outside looks after itself. This is why I don't ever coach a client towards an external goal, without first exploring with them the internal drive and perspective behind this. To simply coach the goal itself is a potentially dangerous pursuit that lacks the awareness and understanding needed to go with it.

Coaching Development

The real power of coaching is never found in change but rather in growth and development. People's capacity to develop themselves in a holistic way, sits at the very heart of coaching. As coaches we must empower our clients to navigate the growing process as best they can, so they are able to fully embrace the whole process of growth and all the fears, gains, losses and unknowns they will encounter along the way.

Chapter 4

Connection - People Grow People

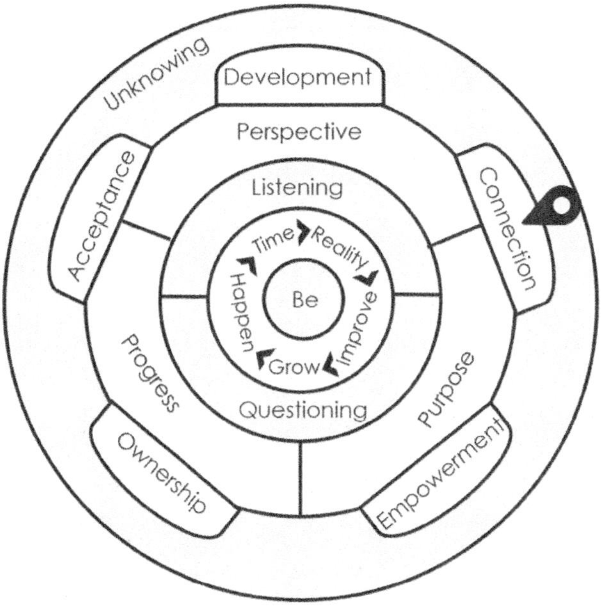

"It is an absolute human certainty that no one can know his own beauty or perceive a sense of his own worth until it has been reflected back to him in the mirror of another loving, caring human being."

John Joseph Powell, The Secret of Staying in Love

Beauty grew the Beast

The Disney version of Beauty and the Beast is often held up as a great romance, where messages like '*love conquers all*' and '*beauty is only skin deep*' are portrayed. Yet, there is a stronger, subtler message running throughout the tale and it's the same story that is played out in many a narrative, from Lord of The Rings to The BFG and from Harry Potter to Good Will Hunting. It's the simple insight that growth and development occur within relationship and connection. The Beast takes Belle, the beautiful young girl from the village, as his prisoner in his castle. As the story unfolds and Belle begins to befriend the Beast's servants, it becomes clear that her presence is also having an impact on the Beast himself. He begins to grow, not because of anything that Belle does for him, but simply because of who she is and how they begin to connect with each other. It's a truth that story tellers throughout the ages have known; relationship and connection spark growth into life. There is nothing more powerful for development to occur, than quality connection. The growth is found in the relationship. It is the connection the Beast feels with Belle that creates the growth in him. Belle doesn't have a fancy programme or course for the Beast, she doesn't offer him treatment, or a 5-step plan and she doesn't even ask him to fill in a personality profile. What she offers him is much more precious that any of those things. She offers herself, her presence and a connection that creates the environment for growth to take place. It's the same thing that Dumbledore offers Harry Potter, the same thing the BFG offers Sophie and the same thing Dr. Sean offers Will Hunting. They offer themselves, a connection, a relationship and a partnership. I have discovered for myself, through decades of working with people, that the greatest and only way to set our innate desire to grow free from the clutter of conditioning, is found in connection and partnership. The upmost help we can be to another person in the aid of their development is to create a quality of connection with them that enables them to tap back into their inbuilt urge to grow.

It was during my years as a youth worker, living and working in one of the toughest inner-cities areas in Britain, that I truly learnt the power of connection and partnership. I realised we could have run as many events, programmes and sessions for these hard-to-reach young people as we liked, and it wouldn't have brought about the slightest ounce of growth. We could have had all-singing, all-dancing packages to offer these kids, where they could be engaged from dawn to dusk in exciting activities and it would not have empowered them to develop themselves, in anyway. Unless everything we did was immersed in partnership and connection, it was ultimately of little worth. Programmes don't grow people; people grow people. Connection with people is what ignites growth, a relationship is the only environment I know of that creates enough safety for people to undertake the real journey of growth. We can deliver all the programmes, courses, talks and even coaching we want, but if they are not steeped firstly in quality human connection, they will only ever pay lip service to development. In all walks of life, from families to education, to the workplace and even the military, it is people and our connections with each other that truly empower us to grow.

As a coach we can learn as many coaching skills as we like, we can practice and hone those skills until the proverbial '*cows come home*', but without connection and partnership, those skills are worthless. Being skilled in communication and coaching means nothing unless we are truly connected with the person in front of us. Therefore, my early efforts in all my coaching work with people, is not about demonstrating my skills or knowledge. It is first and foremost about establishing a quality connection, because I know that without connection, there will never be any real growth.

Belonging

There is something about being human which gives us a deep longing to connect with each other. It's not just about connecting on a superficial level, we long for connections with real depth and substance. Connecting starts from the moment we were born, when we stared into our mother's eyes desperately trying to connect with her, to start the process of creating our first relationship. Since that moment we've never stopped trying to connect and bond with people around us; our siblings, friends, teachers, neighbours, teammates and everyone else in our life. No matter whether our childhood was abundant in love and affection, or missing the care and relationship we deserved, our desire for connection remains. It is part of our human nature. Deep down inside, there is a want to belong, a longing to be attached to people around us, as though it is written in our DNA, at the heart of what it means to be truly human. We are meant to be with other people, we are meant to be relating to one another, it is the most natural thing in the world for us to be doing. Possibly the strongest motivator within us is this desire to belong.

One of the foundations on which coaching must be built is the connection and partnership that exists between the coach and the client. Without a strong connection, coaching will not be effective, no matter how skilled the coach or how willing the client. The partnership that is held between coach and client, is possibly the most crucial element of the whole coaching process. Get it right and it will ignite the coaching but get it wrong and coaching is going nowhere.

Connections we hold with other people are like bridges that link us together. Some bridges we build with others are constructed of nothing more than straw. A small level of connection exists, but there is no great depth or strength to it and at the first sign of any difficulty or heavy load the bridge collapses in an instance. Other bridges we have with people are so powerful, it's as though they are built of iron girders, capable of enduring anything that may pass across them. We hold all levels of connections with people and therefore a variety of bridges differing in strength and weight-bearing ability. In fact, every connection is so unique, we often subconsciously weigh up the strength of the bridge between us before we throw certain words, questions or stories across it. This is the reason two different people could say the same thing to us and in one instance we would be able to take those words on board and in another, we would be deeply offended. It is not so much the words which matter, but rather the strength of the bridge those words are journeying over. As the connection grows and develops in strength, so does the weight of the questions and sharing it can endure. When a bridge between a coach and client is "straw-like", the coaching will never develop past a surface level of conversation. The coach will not be able to ask the truly meaningful questions and the client will not feel safe enough to share the real depth of their heart. When a bridge between a coach and client is made of iron, there is nothing which it cannot bear and the depth of connection which occurs enables the coaching to be effective at a level which surpasses the skill of the coach or the willingness of the client. The connection creates a setting which enables the coaching process to take effect and without that environment the client cannot grow as they perhaps might. I have come to see it is not so much the skill of the coach, the cleverness of their questions, or even the methods and theories they use that truly empower a client towards growth. It is the depth of connection and partnership which exists between coach and client that creates the catalyst for development.

Beliefs About People

The starting point for any connection or partnership to develop begins with our beliefs about people. It is imperative we understand and examine the beliefs we hold in our hearts about people. These beliefs will drive and dictate how we relate and connect to people. Do we believe people are fundamentally good or bad? Are people inherently honest or dishonest? Are people capable or in need of help? All these questions and many more need to be asked of ourselves, in order to ensure there is nothing in our belief system that inadvertently gets in the way of creating helpful partnerships with our clients.

Dave was a young youth worker we recruited to come work alongside some of the most disengaged young people in our community. He was enthusiastic, intelligent and a good communicator. He started well, threw himself into the work and showed real eagerness to learn. Yet after a few months it became apparent that he struggled to build quality relationships with young people. They just couldn't buy into him. To begin with I was baffled. What was it about Dave that was turning young people off? On the surface there was nothing obvious. He had all the attributes we would look for in someone doing his role. However, as I watched and looked deeper, I noticed the subtleties of the situation and in particular, some of the underlying beliefs that Dave held. He had been born and raised in an affluent middle-class family and somehow this had translated into a belief that these inner-city, disenfranchised young people needed rescuing from their lives. Dave felt sorry for them, he saw them as helpless, broken and stuck. He never made any of these statements aloud, but it became clear in his attitude that he saw himself as their rescuer. The young people knew it from the get go. What had taken me months to see, these teenagers had felt instantly, and it made them repel from him. A very subtle underlying belief that Dave would never have dreamed of verbalising, was oozing out of him and being picked up by the young people. It was this simple belief that was hindering any chance of quality connection. Until Dave was able to rework this belief and see these young people as okay, capable and partners he would never develop the kind of connection needed to help them grow.

In every connection I create with a coaching client I make every conscious attempt to start with the belief that we are equals. I never see them as broken, helpless or in need of rescue. They might feel like they're carrying a few bruises, but they are not broken. We are simply partners in the process. I am not their life guru, saviour or rescuer, I am their companion and they are mine, as we walk this journey together.

Rapport to Relationship to Robustness

Connections can be incredibly complex. To help us understand a coaching partnership I have simplified and broken it down into three levels of depth. True connections have a flow that begin with rapport, develop into relationship and then deepen into robustness. It is a process to be aware of if we want to create healthy, balanced and effective partnerships.

Every connection between two human beings begins with rapport. Consider the strongest, deepest friendships we now hold in our lives. At some point these were once little more than just rapport. Even in the family relationships we were born into with parents and siblings there was a moment, however briefly, where there was only rapport present. At some point this initial connection moved beyond rapport and became something which took the form of a stronger relationship. Then perhaps, over time the relationship developed to a depth of complete and utter robustness, where we became free to say anything to each other, or not speak for months and the level of connection and intimacy remained constant. This same process occurs between coach and client. Obviously confined by very different professional boundaries than a friendship, yet the coach/client connection still flows through the same process of rapport to relationship to robustness. It is vital as a coach to be conscious of this process and understand the attributes required to ensure the connection is enhancing and helpful to the coaching process.

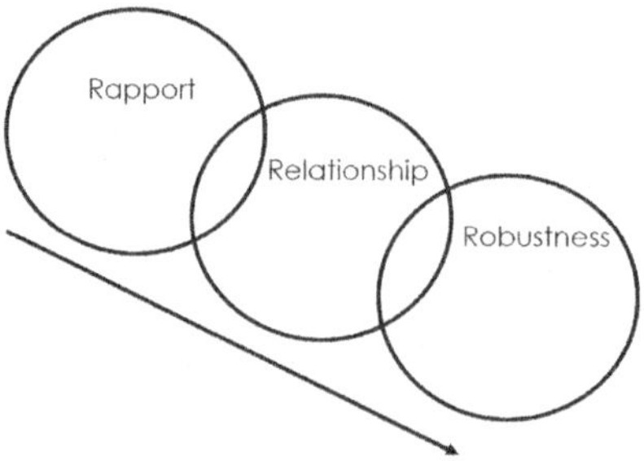

In day to day life, not all connections develop past rapport, in fact some never even make it into rapport. There is a disconnect between the people involved that stops rapport from ever beginning. Yet even if rapport is found, it certainly doesn't mean the connection will go any further than that. It is possible to remain in a state of rapport with another person for years and even decades, where the connection never delves any deeper than the level of small talk, banter or common interest. In our lives, rapport connections are often our acquaintances. They are the people with whom our paths cross and we know well enough to hold a conversation with, but there is no depth to our relationship with them. They range from the people we say “hello” to when we pass in the street, to members of our social circle we chat with, but don’t really know in any depth. These kinds of connections operate on the surface, yet we mustn’t down play the importance of rapport because it is one of the most crucial attributes a coach can offer their client in the early stages of a coaching connection.

Rapport

Rapport is a difficult word to describe. It is much more of something we feel rather than something we think. The English language is limited in its ability to convey what this initial connection between two human beings is, hence why we have borrowed the French word “rapport”. It is often referred to as the chemistry, the spark, the warmth or the comfortableness you may feel when meeting someone for the first time. However, we often become most aware of it in its absence. Those moments we find ourselves in a social situation and we are unsure what to say, or how to spark conversation, there is an awkwardness that prevails, which is the antithesis of rapport. Yet when we find a level of rapport with another, there is something which feels so natural, so comfortable it's as though we are not even trying. We just seem to connect in a way which belies the short amount of time spent together.

Many people believe rapport is something that just happens. You either click with someone or you don't. It's true as a coach you may click easier with some people than others, but it is still possible to build rapport with anyone who is willing to build rapport with you. Although, it isn't simply about learning a specific set of rapport building skills. Many people have written about the skills involved in rapport building; such as finding common ground, listening, making eye contact and having an open posture. Yet these, along with a whole list of other skills, are simply the mechanics of rapport building. They are skills which can be taught to and learnt by anyone and yet even with these skills in their toolbox some people still find real rapport building a difficult process. This is because these skills are only what is visible and happening on the surface, whereas when rapport truly takes place it is happening under the surface in an invisible way. I am not saying that these skills are not necessary, but they are not the essence of building rapport, they are simply the result. They are what people notice when rapport is taking place, but they are not what truly makes rapport happen. It would be a bit like believing all you need to be a world-class artist is a canvas, a brush and different coloured paint. Yet true artists create art, not so much from the tools at their disposal, but rather with the flair and creativity that lies within them. The essence of real rapport building begins much deeper than the surface skills. In fact, it starts with things that are not skills at all; they are character traits such as passion, curiosity, care, empathy, integrity, love and openness. In coaching, the building of rapport, the forging of a connection is so much more about who you are at your very core, than it ever will be about a set of surface skills.

If rapport remains just a set of skills, it is in danger of taking on the form of faked, inauthentic rapport. The kind of rapport we're on the receiving end of from a salesperson, who has learned a certain set of rapport building skills to ultimately lure us into making a purchase. The car salesman who wants to talk about our family, our home or the uncanny common ground we might share over our love of the same music. The travel agent who always claims they have just returned from the same destination we're looking to book. We can smell this kind of rapport a mile off and it does nothing to forge a connection, in fact it snaps any connection we may have had in two. These people are adept in the skills of rapport building and hone these abilities day after day and on many occasions achieve the desired result. However, as coaches we are not and never should be in the business of using rapport building for our own benefit. It must be about a desire to connect and form partnerships with our clients because they are deserving of our attention and time. We must have a truly authentic want to connect with our clients because we care about them, even if they have only just walked through the door. Interestingly, when we care deeply for our clients in this way, we unwittingly begin to display all the other "skills" of rapport building. We make eye contact, we hold an open posture, we listen, we mirror their body language, we begin to find common ground and we smile.

Relationship to Robustness

As any connection deepens so does the level of trust, vulnerability and honesty that exists between the people involved. By looking again at our own deep friendships, we discover the same elements that need to occur to progress from rapport to a deeper relationship with our clients. It comes down to establishing trust. This begins firstly with us as coaches providing a sense of safety and freedom for our clients. This in turn empowers our clients to be courageous enough to display some vulnerability and honesty, which then enables us to respond again with safety and freedom and perhaps a little vulnerability of our own, which empowers yet deeper vulnerability and honesty from the client. Mix this in with the process of time and consistency and connections begin to move forward and deepen. This process doesn't just happen once, it occurs continually throughout the coaching relationship, like walking downwards on a spiral staircase to new levels of depth and trust. Where with each interaction the bridge of the connection grows stronger and stronger. Once this process has passed through enough cycles, the relationship enters a new stage of robustness, where the trust is steadfast, where vulnerability and honesty along with safety and freedom become the norms of the partnership between coach and client. What a place of beauty that is, to experience such sincerity with another. This is where the real magic of coaching happens, in a connection of utter robustness where the client can explore and wrestle and reflect in such a way that growth simply flows forward from them.

As we move through each stage of this connection with our clients, we must carry some of the previous stages with us. Rapport is just as important in a place of robustness as it is in the beginning. In many marriages or long-term relationships, it is easy to see a couple reach a stage where they have arrived at absolute robustness, but somewhere along the way they lost the rapport, the spark, the fun. To have truly healthy, effective connections we need to arrive in a place of deep robustness, with both rapport and relationship still burning brightly.

Who the Coach is

Clients will connect with different parts of us as coaches and each of these parts determine the strength of the connection. We need to take a good look at ourselves and who we really are at each of these levels, to understand the connections we create. Who we really are is the vital element to the establishing of quality connections and partnership with clients. I don't mean this in the sense of our name, role or social standing. I mean who we are at our very core, who we are in the very essence of our being. When it comes to creating real connection and ultimately growth, as a coach, who we are is so much more important than anything we do. Many people approach coaching with the belief that it can be learnt through acquiring knowledge of a few skills and techniques. That belief is dangerous. Quality coaches are not simply trained, they are forged through a life-long process of learning, experience, enlightenment, reflection and personal development. There are some skills that can be improved, honed and sharpened over time, but it runs so much deeper. Acquiring coaching skills is not enough in itself. There is a depth to being a great coach that must be appreciated and understood. Some people hold virtually all the attributes of a great coach without ever having been taught a single skill, whilst others can have coaching qualifications in abundance, but still struggle to deliver great coaching. I always encourage coaches to practice their skills, but I urge them even more to develop who they are. Ultimately people grow people, so who we are is the key component of truly successful connections.

The Layers of Connection

As coaches we are like Russian Dolls with layers of ourselves, under layers of ourselves. We have so many layers at so many levels it would be too complex, diverse and messy to try to make sense of them all. For the sake of simplicity, I have grouped us into three layers; our image, our personality and our character.

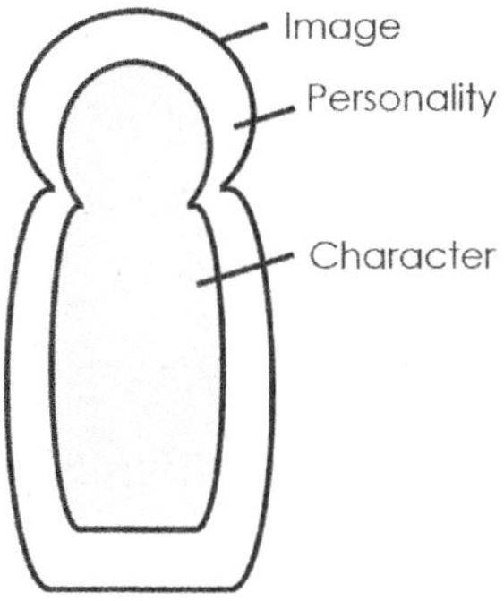

Image

Our image is perhaps the first thing our clients may notice, it is the first part of us that they may be attracted to or repel from. It is right there on the outside for the entire world to see. Our image consists of our appearance, our experience, our qualifications, our branding, our social media presence, even perhaps our easily demonstrable skills and knowledge, and anything else that can be seen immediately by the world around us.

Our clients may notice whether as coaches we look the part, sound like we know what we are doing, possess skills they would deem desirable, have an attractive brand and seem professional. Image is often the layer on which people focus the most attention. I've seen many coaches work incredibly hard on their image and brand because they know we sadly live in an image driven culture. They believe the better their image, the more money they will make. Unfortunately, some parts of our image are important in order to create a good first impression or capture people's interest, so they stick around long enough to find out more. It is imperative, as coaches, that we are continually enhancing our skills, knowledge and experience, but there is so much more needed than image alone. Image is the most fragile and brittle of all the layers because it is just the front screen, the outer skin that doesn't take much to be completely broken in an instant. We only have to look at the lives of celebrities, where overnight one news headline immediately destroys the image they may have worked tireless over decades to create. Image is also the part of us where we can potentially be the most inauthentic. It is quite straight forward in our modern age to create a great image that actually has very little substance to back it up. We can produce pictures, write ups and even testimonials of ourselves that make our image desirable to potential clients. However, without the backing of a quality personality, and even more so, quality character, then our image is just a façade that will not enable our clients to have the connection with us that empowers their growth. Coaching is dangerous when it is too reliant on the image a coach has created because it lacks the depth of connection our clients truly need and deserve. When a client connects with a coach only on an image level, (in the sense that the client buys into the coach purely from a place of appearance, qualifications, branding or the skills they can demonstrate) it creates a brittle connection that can be easily broken. The bridge between them is weak and so it produces a partnership where true challenge, real honesty and strong questions cannot be offered and received. There isn't the security, safety and vulnerability needed to empower real growth.

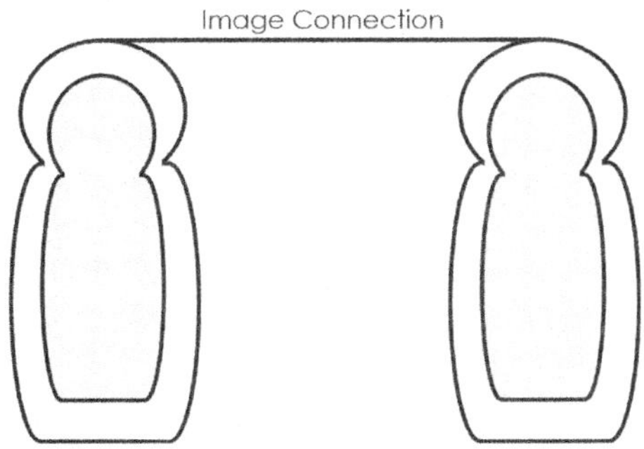

Personality

Our personality is the part of us that we show outwardly. It is the part of us that is loud or quiet, outgoing or reserved, upbeat or dour, funny or serious, optimistic or pessimistic. It's the us we can flex, moderate or control, depending upon the situations we find ourselves in. Coaches, like all people, can bend and arch their personality to suit certain situations and circumstances. It can be helpful to have the ability to flex the different parts of our personalities to suit the differing needs of our clients. In this way we can create a greater range of clients we can work with and offer them more of what they need to create a powerful connection. I'm not in any way suggesting we should be false or fake with our clients. Our personality must always be authentic and real, otherwise clients will eventually realise it is nothing more than a projection. However, our personalities offer us the opportunity to turn up or turn down certain aspects of ourselves in the service of our clients. With some clients my humorous personality comes forth, whereas with others my serious side takes more of the lead. With some I am louder and with others I am quieter. All these parts of me are real, I just mirror my clients' needs by turning up or down the parts of my personality they need more or less of. In society, we often place great importance on personality. As a coach, it certainly has a part to play in building deeper connections with people. When the connection deepens past the initial image to that of personality, then the coaching can deepen with it. The bridge of the connection between the coach and the client can withstand more authenticity and discovery can be expanded, but it is still not the most important layer. Image and personality can help develop and carry a connection so far, but more is needed because partnership and connection truly find their full force when client and coach connect on a character level.

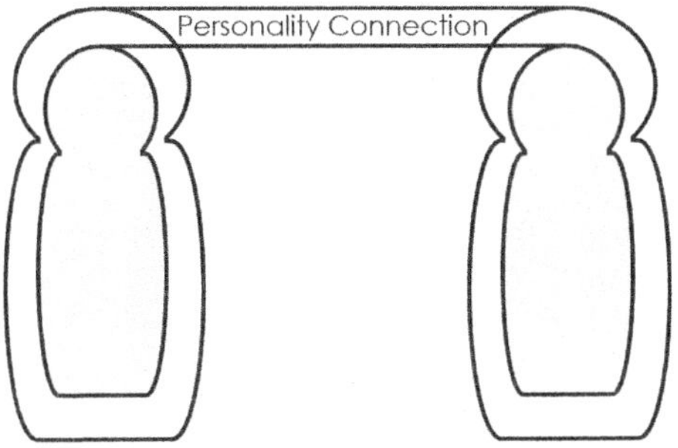

Character

Our character is who we are at our very core. Our character is where we find our values, ethics and principles. Character is the bedrock of who a person is and ultimately how they will be. Character is where honesty, faithfulness, respect, resilience, determination, integrity, fairness, faith and a host of other characteristics are found. Character is not something that can be manipulated or changed, as easily as personality can. Character is forged over a life time and can only be grown and developed slowly. Character is what we find when everything else has been stripped away. It is a person's character we see when they experience great troubles in life or great success.

When image is lacking, and personality is rocked, character remains. Like an anchor at the very soul of a person, character is unwavering. Characteristics such as truth, faithfulness, fairness, respect, discipline, determination and faith are what we find below the surface of a person. They are the facets which emerge the more we get to know someone. It is important to recognise it takes time to really see someone's character; it is not always obvious at first glance what their character is. Many people can do a great job of covering their character with a strong image and big personality and it is all too easy to be duped into believing a person is someone they are not. I have made this mistake many times, but I have also learnt, if we are open to looking for someone's character it is possible over time to see it clearly. If we want to know the true character a person possesses, we must watch how they behave during times of extreme in life. When they are in a position of great power or great weakness, when they are very rich or very poor or when they are being very successful or failing greatly. In these times, we will see people's character and the rawness of their very essence. Quality of character is the most important asset a coach can possess. It far outweighs skills, knowledge, experience and personality. Character is where all the qualities that ultimately create an empowering partnership, are found. Trust, love, faith, hope and openness are all found in a person's character. These are not skills or personality traits, they are characteristics that enable a quality of connection that in turn unlocks people's potential to grow. When clients connect with coaches at a character level, it happens way below the surface of anything visible. It is a connection so strong that it can bear the weight of any conversation that may take place, but this can only happen when both the client and coach are being authentic.

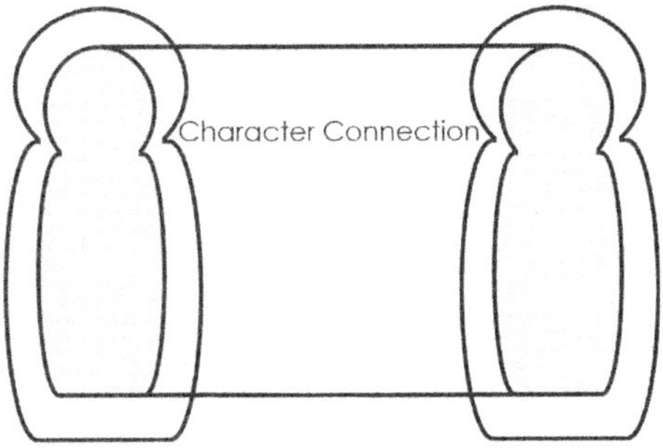

Being Authentically You

True quality of connection only happens when people are authentic. When the facades, smokescreens and personas are dropped, and the parties connect on a truly genuine level. Carl Rogers referred to this as 'congruence' and it was one of his core conditions which he believed needed to be present for growth to happen. The difficulty with being our authentic self, is we are often unaware when we are not being. We have grown up in societies and cultures that bombard us with lessons on how we should be, and we lose touch with who we truly are. We are taught which emotions are acceptable and unacceptable to feel. Which behaviours are okay or not okay. Which words are suitable or unsuitable in any given situation. We are so steeped in this image of who we think we should be, that we lose sight of who we really are. This idea of being our authentic self or congruent makes perfect sense in theory and yet in reality, is an almighty challenge. It is something which constantly stretches me. I have spent many times being utterly incongruent and yet believing I was being truly authentic; in a sense of denial about my true feelings or thoughts, whilst projecting outwardly an acceptable set of emotions or behaviours. It is a complete minefield of reflection, self-awareness and understanding. I could tie myself in knots attempting to be my authentic self and yet I have concluded the best I can do is to be as authentic as I possibly can, in any given situation. For me, this means letting my character, personality and image line up in a way that connects with each other. Where there is no disjoint between them, that my image isn't hiding my personality, that my personality isn't protecting my character. Instead, there is openness to all these parts of me, there is an authenticity and genuineness in all of me. When I am not being authentic there is disharmony between my character, personality and image. It is as though my character believes one thing and yet my image portrays something else. My values have been rocked and yet my personality smooths it over. Authenticity flows from me when my character, personality and image are in perfect harmony. I'm not suggesting coaches have to have perfect, flawless images, personalities and characters, no-one does. It's not about looking for perfection as a coach. We all have flaws of one kind or another, we all have blemishes. As a coach it's about being able to look honestly at who we are and be prepared to let that show, all of it. Not falling into the trap of simply projecting an image or personality we want people to buy into. It is about being authentic in who we are.

One of the ways I reflect on my level of authenticity with my clients, is to ask how they would react if they saw other parts of my life. If any of my clients were to witness me in my home, or out with my friends, or on holiday, would they be surprised by what they saw? Or would they see the same person they know in the coaching room? This doesn't mean that I disclose every part of my life to my clients, far from it. The connection is for their benefit, not mine, but I do make every attempt to take my authentic self with me into those partnerships. I believe people buy into my coaching because of who I am, more than anything I do or don't do. It is vital that our clients get the whole of us as coaches. Our image, personality and character all go with us into the coaching room and it is vital they are all authentically present in their own way. If I could teach only one thing to trainee coaches, it would be the ability to be with their clients in such a way that it creates deep, authentic connections. Everything else there is to learn about coaching, is secondary to the relationship held between coach and client. Carl Rogers summed this up beautifully, *"In my early professional years I was asking the question: How can I treat, or cure, or change this person? Now I would phrase the question in this way: How can I provide a relationship which this person may use for his own personal growth?"*

Chapter 5

Empowerment: Faith, Hope and Love

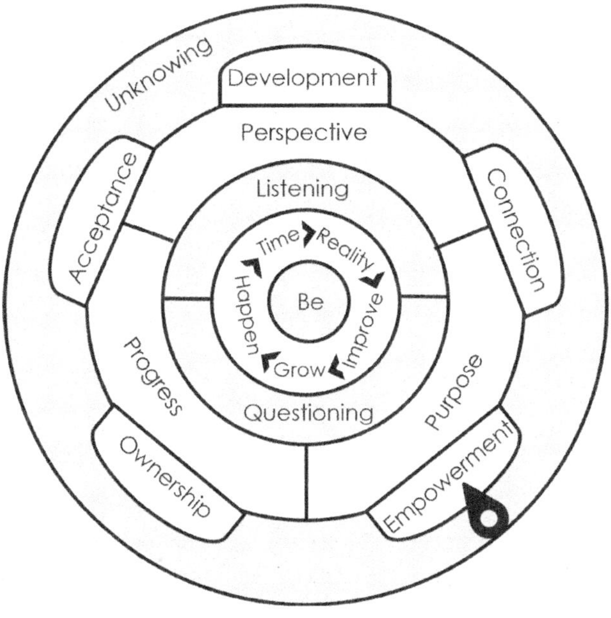

"The three most important things to have are faith, hope and love. But the greatest of them is love."

1 Corinthians 13:12-13

The Hiding Place

There is a story within Hindu tradition that tells of a time when all human beings were gods, but they abused that divinity to such an extent that Brahma, the creator God, decided to remove it from them and hide it somewhere humans would never be able to find it.

Brahma called a meeting of all the gods to help him decide where to hide this divinity from humankind. “Bury it deep under the earth,” said the gods. “No,” responded Brahma, “That won’t work, because humans will dig down into the earth and find it one day.

”Then the gods suggested, “Sink it in the deepest of the oceans.” “No,” replied Brahma once more, “that will not do, because humans will one day learn to dive into the ocean and find it there.”

Then the gods said, “Take it to the highest mountain peak and leave it there.” “No” responded Brahma once more, “humans will scale every mountain and take up their divinity once more.”

The gods gave up and said, “We don’t know where to hide it, because there seems no place on earth that humans will not eventually reach.”

Brahma thought for a long time and eventually spoke, "Here is what we will do. We will hide their divinity in the one place that humans will never think to look. We will hide it deep within the centre of their own being."

All the gods agreed that this was the ideal place and so the deed was done. Since that day humans have been digging, diving and climbing in pursuit of something that already lies within them.

What is Empowerment?

Empowerment is simply the rising and increase in power, control and influence that we feel. We so often go seeking this empowerment from people and places outside of ourselves, and yet, like divinity in the Hindu tradition, true empowerment can only be found within us. Often, empowerment is thought to be the idea of one person giving power to another, where one person gives authority or inspiration to another to take more power of their situation or circumstances. People often look for empowerment in external sources such as authority figures, motivational speakers or inspiring quotes and yet true empowerment only ever comes from inside us.

This is the reason that within coaching there is no sense of a coach giving power to a client. It is not the case that a coach gives authority or inspiration to a client to take more power. In coaching, empowerment comes from inside of the client themselves. No power is given to them by the coach, it is found within them raising and expanding the power they already possess. As coaches we must believe all people have power hidden within them, even if that power has been squashed and covered and remained unused for years, it is still there. It may take our clients a while to acknowledge the power within and even longer to allow it to rise, but it is most certainly there. True empowerment is never given to a person, it is grown from the power they already have in their possession. It is not the coach's job to empower our clients, it is simply our role to offer the most helpful environment we can for our clients to explore and discover their own power.

I'm aware that 'power' is a provocative word, that often conjures images of lightning bolts or oppressive leadership, but this isn't my meaning of the word. Sometimes power can be quiet and even subtle, it can be the simple discovery of having greater choice over a situation or of gaining clarity or focus. Empowerment works on many different levels for each individual person. Sometimes it comes in an instant, like a great revelation, at other times it creeps gradually like an incoming tide.

The Different Soil of Coaching

For a coach it is simply about providing the best environment in which our clients can be empowered. Dave Mearns and Brian Thorne in their work in Person-Centred Therapy refer to this as providing *"different soil"* in which the client can begin to grow. I love the idea that a coaching relationship provides a different soil in which people can grow, because it must be a connection unlike any other relationship people hold in their lives. Most human relationships come with a set of rules, boundaries and circumstances and they are held by invisible, unspoken conditions, that warp or squash the people in them. Coaches must strive to create relationships that create a freedom and flow, that enable unhindered conversations to take place, where people are liberated to talk and explore who they really are, what they really want and where they truly want to go.

Over the years, in my quest to understand what it is that most helps my clients to find and feel empowered, I have reached no new conclusion or revolutionary discovery. Instead, I have returned to an ancient truth, that empowerment is found within the security of three things, faith, hope and love. It is these three elements that must be ever present within the coaching connection. It is within their presence that empowerment takes place, because it is faith, hope and love that create the ingredients in which empowerment thrives.

Empowerment comes when we are able to find more autonomy in our choices and decisions. When we begin to live lives on the outside that are in line with our inner thoughts and feelings. When we are able to make conscious choices about our lives it is through faith, hope and love that this takes place. We feel empowered when we have faith in ourselves to make decisions and take action, when we have hope that there is more within us and we are greater than we even know, and when we have love for the whole of ourselves, not just the good bits.

As coaches it is our role to model faith, hope and love to our clients by offering it to them in every interaction, in every part of our relationship with them and with every essence of our being.

Faith

Having faith means to place our trust and belief wholeheartedly in something or someone. We display great feats of faith each day of our lives. We have faith in our cars to start in the morning, we trust the chairs we sit on to bear our weight, we believe in elevator doors to open and yet when it comes to other people and ourselves, we can find our faith lacking.

Empowerment starts with people finding faith in themselves. To believe in ourselves and our own judgements is a wonderfully empowering place to be. I work with so many people who simply don't trust that what they are doing, how they are living and that the choices they are making are OK. They are forever looking for affirmation from the world around them that they are on the right track and this constant need for external confirmation, robs them of their certainty and ultimately disempowers them.

As coaches we can help people be empowered by simply having faith in them. Having faith sounds easy, trusting someone completely is surely straight forward enough and holding belief in someone must be a natural process for us. Yet, faith is so often lacking within our societies, trust is regularly missing in our day-to-day relationships and belief in people isn't the norm. I see so much doubt in the world, so much cynicism and suspicion in other people that we have become used to only offering a half-faith, a bit of our trust, but not utter unadulterated belief in people. Even within the closest, most intimate relationships between parent and child, husband and wife or long-term friends, I see mistrust and doubt. To be offered faith by another person, to be trusted completely is a wonderful sensation that grows and expands any power we already possess within us.

There are three areas we need to have faith within coaching. We must have faith in who our client is, faith in their ability to find their way forward and faith in the coaching process itself.

Faith in who they are

Empowerment can grow or shrink from the faith and trust that others have in us because we tend to live up or down to the belief placed in us. We see this in children, that they regularly live up or down to the expectations placed on them by the adults in their lives. It's as though we reflect the faith being placed in us. I know this from my own sporting career. If I had a team manager who believed in me and rated me, I would live up to those expectations and more often than not, perform well. If I was playing for someone who didn't believe in me as a player, I would find it difficult to produce my best form. Faith places a major role in our feelings of empowerment and as coaches we have the wonderful opportunity to believe in our clients, to have faith in who they are, to trust them.

Trusting someone completely was once straight forward enough for most of us, because when it comes to faith, the greatest distributors in our society are children. They trust in such a beautifully naïve way. They have faith in people. They look beyond the external appearance and place their belief in who the person is. Somewhere along the line we lost this and began to doubt people. We became cynical, suspicious and uncertain with people. We replaced faith with misgiving. Yet, if we are to help people discover their own power, we must learn to have faith again like little children, believing in the greatness within people. We must be able to offer our clients faith and trust in a way that shouts to them "I believe in you", in every interaction we have with them. We must believe that they are OK, they are capable, and they are good enough. In this way, we offer them something they rarely find in the world around them. Usually they are only offered faith by people they have proved themselves to over and over again. Within coaching, I have faith in my clients from the first moment with them. I trust them because they are human, and I believe in the greatness that exists within all of us. My clients don't have to win my faith, they don't have to earn my trust, it is offered freely to them.

Faith in their ability to find their own way

We must have faith in our clients to find their own way, to work it out for themselves. When we have this unwavering faith in our client, we have no need to rescue them or lead them anywhere. There is simply a trust that silently communicates, "You've got this," "You can handle it," "You can find your way." To be trusted is one of the highest motivators for humans. When we are trusted we feel empowered to achieve, we feel capable. Even when our clients are stuck or going around in circles, our faith in them must not waver. We must hold true to the trust we have that they can and will figure it out.

It was early on in my coaching career, whilst working with Lucy, that I really learnt to trust my clients to find their own way. Lucy wasn't a CEO or well-educated adult, she wasn't a parent or leader in anyway. Lucy was a nine-year-old girl. She had been referred for coaching because her teachers and parents felt she would benefit from growing her self-confidence. On first meeting, it was clear there was something going on for her. She was visibly nervous and for the first session barely said a word. As our sessions went on, bit by bit, she began to talk a little more. When I asked her what other people had told her about her confidence, she really began to open up, saying she had been advised to walk confidently, to tell herself positive things, to think positive thoughts and to actively make friends, but that none of this had helped her at all. So, I asked her a simple question, "What would you tell yourself to do?" Her answer almost bowled me off my chair.

"Oh, I know exactly what I need to do," came her response. Here was a timid, nine-year-old girl with more advice from adults than she could carry, who knew exactly what to do. Her response showed me the importance of trusting my clients' ability to find their own way. If I had set about offering advice it would have been nothing she hadn't heard before and if I had tried to lead her down a path, it certainly wouldn't have gone where we were about to go.

"It's really simple but scary," she continued. "All I need to do is start to put my hand up in class. I really can't do it because I'm so scared of getting the answer wrong, even when I know the answer. If I could put my hand up, I know that I would be more confident." That was it, the moment that I fully bought into the faith that my clients can find their own way. It's so simple and straight forward, yet it was not an answer that anyone else in Lucy's life would have ever offered her, including me.

The change I saw in Lucy over the coming weeks was phenomenal. She set herself daily challenges to put her hand up in class and she surpassed each and every one of them. She was right, her confidence did grow and it was a privilege to witness. I had done nothing for this girl, other than offer her one question that demonstrated my faith in her ability to find her own way. She grabbed that faith by the hand and ran with it to a place I couldn't have dreamed of getting to.

We must trust our clients to find their own way and when we do, their own way is remarkable.

Faith in the coaching process

I trust the coaching process completely. I know it works, I have seen it deliver time and again and during our coaching training courses I regularly remind the trainees to 'trust the process'. It's incredibly difficult for a client to trust the coaching process if, we as coaches, don't have faith in it.

It's in the moments when our clients seem to be struggling to find their way, or the coaching gets stuck, or the conversation seems to have headed down a dead end, or our clients aren't moving forward. It's in these moments where our faith in the process wins out.

In coaching it can sometimes feel like our clients are going backwards, that coaching is making things worse and that it just isn't working. In these moments, trust the process. It is all part of the journey and sometimes it's exactly where our client needs to be. At times its OK that a coaching session gets stuck, or feels a bit dry, this is often a place on the journey that our clients need to be for a while. Let it be and trust the process. As soon as we lose faith in the process, we start to disempower our clients and we tend to return to what we have known previously. We start to mentor or offer advice. We start to feel like we need to rescue the session. A sure sign of this is when we start to do more of the talking than our client. Our clients will look to us in these moments and if our faith is unwavering in the coaching process, then theirs will be too. They will be able to relax and find their own faith in what is taking place. They will be able to feel empowered by the interaction that is happening and trust themselves to grow in the way that is right for them.

Hope

There is a sense within our modern western culture of hope being something more like wishful thinking, a sense of crossing our fingers and 'hoping' that something good might happen. People talk about their 'hope' in winning the lottery, their 'hope' that the sun will shine at the weekend and their 'hope' that their favourite sports team will be victorious. Yet hope has a different sense within other cultures. Within Jewish tradition there are two kinds of hope. One is the hope that light will prevail over darkness, that good will come, even though it might not look exactly as we'd wish. The other hope is a certainty in something better, that we know will surely come. It might seem strange to talk of hope with certainty, but this kind of hope is not the wishful thinking kind. This hope is more of an anticipation for what we know will come to pass. It is a hope that expects rather than wishes and it is this kind of hope I believe we must have in our clients. A hope that knows there is more in them, there is better available for them, there is greatness within them that lies undiscovered. None of this is a 'cross-your-fingers and hope for the best' kind of hope. It is a hope with assurance, a hope in people that has certainty with it. In this sense, I have hope that I will always love my wife, I have hope that my children will grow to be good people, I have hope that I will handle 'it', whatever 'it' may be. There is a certainty within this hope.

Empowerment rises when people place this kind of hope in us. We have the privileged position as coaches to be able to offer this hope to our clients, so that they may be able to capture this hope and find it within themselves also. It is a hope for their present circumstances, a hope for their future, a hope that they are more than they believe they are, a hope that they can clear out the rubbish and a hope that they can embrace their true self. We can never lose hope in and for our clients, as soon as we do, we disempower them, we dent their own hope. We must offer hope to our clients even in the most challenging of circumstances. It is in these moments that they need to know and feel that our hope in and for them is unwavering.

Love

It may seem extreme to suggest that as coaches we must love our clients, but we must, because love is the greatest. There is nothing I know of that usurps love. It is the highest of all entities and it always wins out, it always finds a way. It is the most empowering factor that exists within human relationships. Nothing compels us and pulls us like love. However, we must understand the kind of love we are talking about because the English language can hinder our understanding of love. I can say, "I love my children" and I can also say "I love ice cream". How can that be the same word? The meaning and feeling bestowed to 'love' in those sentences are radically different. In Ancient Greek there are at least four different words to describe different types of love. Although it can be difficult to fully conceive each of these outside of their original contexts, it can be helpful to our understanding of 'love' to have an idea of their meanings. In Ancient Greek, 'Eros' is the intimate, sexual, passionate love we have for another person, 'Philia' is the love between friends, like a brotherly or sisterly love for one another, 'Storge' is the love that exists within family relationships and 'Agape' is the sense of unconditional love and self-sacrificing love.

CS Lewis told us, *"So there are 4 kinds of 'love,' all good in their proper place, but Agape is the best because it is the kind God has for us and is good in all circumstances. There are people I mustn't feel Eros towards and people I can't feel Storge or Philia for; but I can practice Agape to God, Angels, Man and Beast, to the good and the bad, the old and the young, the far and the near. You see Agape is all giving, not getting."* Agape is a pure love that asks nothing of the person in return. It loves, simply because people are worth loving and it expects nothing back. It is agape that best describes the type of love I believe we must have for our clients.

Carl Rogers in his Person-Centred model proposed we most hold our clients in something he referred to as 'Unconditional Positive Regard'. It was one of the core conditions he believed must be offered and received for people to develop. It is a sense of always, no matter what, seeing our clients in a positive light. Although I agree with Rogers' idea of it being unconditional, I don't think positive regard goes far enough. It is love we must be offering our clients, it is agape. This unconditional love that nothing you can tell me or do, makes you unworthy or blemished. It is not a love that says, "if you behave or speak in a certain way, only then are you acceptable," it is a love that says, "every part of you is loveable in every way." This can prove a challenge to us as coaches because we will coach people who hold different views of the world, different values and ethics. They will put our agape on trial in various ways, but we must be unwavering in our offering of this love to our clients.

This doesn't mean we must continue to coach people with whom we feel uncomfortable and it doesn't mean we negate our responsibility to keep watch over safeguarding issues or risks posed by clients. There is still a professional standard and ethic we must adhere to as coaches, but we must love people and even in our uncomfortableness or professional responsibility it is possible to love. To be loved and accepted is the greatest need and want of all humans and as coaches we are given a privileged opportunity and set of circumstances in which we can offer agape to our clients.

Empowerment begins when we are loved unconditionally. When we are able to be completely and utterly ourselves, without the loss of love or the withdrawing of approval, there is a sense of power that rises within us. There is nothing I know of more empowering than love. We see this vividly in our schools amongst our children. Nicholas Ferroni, the influential American educator famously said, *"Students who are loved at home come to school to learn. Those who aren't, come to school to be loved."*

When we are loved, we begin the process of empowerment, but when we are able to truly love ourselves, we experience abounding empowerment. Being loved by another is critical for us but being able to discover our own self-love is where empowerment really flourishes. It is agape, unconditional love, that we must learn to offer to ourselves. As coaches, by offering agape to our clients, we again model a process that hopefully over time they adopt and apply for themselves.

Coaching Empowerment

Empowerment is found deep within ourselves and we cannot ever push another person towards empowerment or force them to feel empowered. All we can do is offer them our faith, our hope and our love and in this way quietly show them the way towards their own empowerment. It is in this way of being with our clients that we create a "different soil" in which they can grow. In our offering of faith, hope and love we also offer them the opportunity to find empowerment deep within the centre of their own being.

Chapter 6

Ownership – Finding the Balance

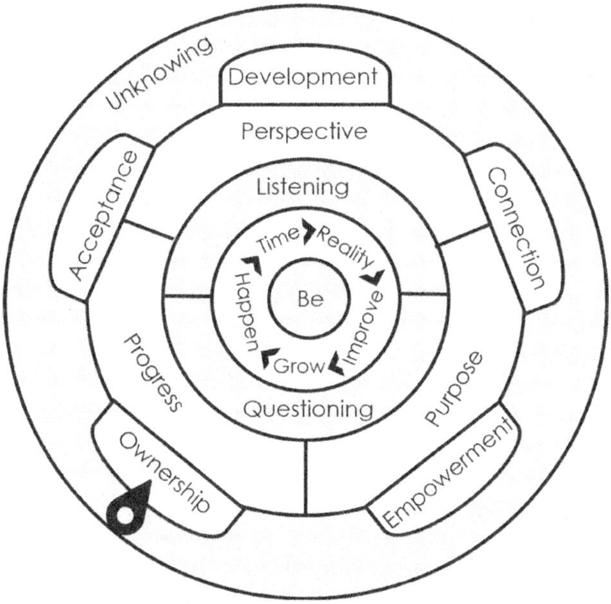

"Jack and Jill went up the hill to fetch a pail of water
So they say, their subsequent fall was inevitable
They never stood a chance; they were written that way
Innocent victims of their story."

Tim Minchin, Naughty, Matilda the Musical

Know Your Zone

How much of our life stories are inevitable and how much of it we can shape ourselves, depends on both the set of circumstances that happen to us and our attitudes to ownership.

“Stay in your zone”, she shouted for the umpteenth time. “You can’t go in that area,” she instructed once more. “Don’t stop, you’re allowed in there”, came her encouraging words over and over. As she repeated her instructions yet again, I was starting to feel sorry for my daughter’s netball coach, as the first match this team of six-year-olds had ever played began to descend into chaos. As these kids were trying to get to grips with where they were and weren’t allowed to be on court, the coach maintained her relentless belief that they were making progress. Netball is the ultimate team sport. With seven players on each side, it isn’t one of those games where the star player can win a match virtually single-handedly, because in netball each player has specific zones of the court that they can and can’t enter. This means the centre court players aren’t allowed in the shooting area, the goal shooter can’t enter the centre court; wing defence cannot enter the attacking third and so on. What this creates, is a sport where each player is wholly reliant on the other team members to play their part and take responsibility in their own area of the court. For netballers this creates a real dichotomy between the zones in which they can take ownership for their own performance and the areas where they have virtually no influence over the game at all. When my daughter started to play netball, it was fascinating to see these little children trying to make sense of these zonal boundaries. In their first match they were not just overstepping the boundaries but charging full-steam ahead into areas they weren't allowed. At other times, they stopped dead at a line on the floor that they were, in fact, allowed to cross. There would be centre court players taking shots from outside the shooting arc, defensive players in the attacking third and attacking players in the defensive third. In was chaotic, hilarious and rewarding to witness. As I watched this embryonic netball match unfold, it reminded me that the game of netball bears many resemblances to our wider lives. We too wrestle with zonal boundaries within our lives, struggling to understand the areas of life in which we can take ownership and the areas that are simply outside of our influence.

In order to progress and grow, we must be able to understand our own level of ownership for our lives. We must have an ongoing awareness of ownership, because it is imperative to our happiness and success in life. Yet, we very rarely get it right. The difficulty for us, is that to take ownership means to take responsibility, and to let go of ownership means to relinquish control. We so often find ourselves over stepping the mark at both ends of ownership, we don't take enough ownership of circumstances we could change and yet we also don't let go of situations over which we have no control at all.

When we were first born, we had virtually no ownership over our lives. The adults around us made all the decisions for us, good or bad. Then, as toddlers, we started in very small ways to make some choices of our own and began the process of taking a tiny amount of ownership for our lives. As a child and then a teenager, our level of ownership grew more and more, as we were given the freedom to make decisions of our own. As we have grown, so has the level of ownership we have in our life. In adulthood, we are the ones who now have the ownership and yet so many of us struggle to make the adjustment to having this degree of choice. We grew so accustomed to being told what we should do, that when it comes to having the space to make our own decisions, it is something we find difficult to get right. Having said that, we must also acknowledge there are parts of our lives which even as adults, we have no ownership over whatsoever. Life just throws some experiences in our direction and we no longer have other adults to hide behind, it is us who must deal with it and find ways to respond. It's about what we create with what we have been given and the level of ownership we take. Just as netballers must understand the areas of the court in which they can and can't affect the game, so we must comprehend the areas of life in which we can and can't take ownership. Life is a strange mix of what we can make happen and the things that happen to us.

What You Can and Can't Own

Steven Covey presents the idea of us all having a circle of concern and a circle of influence. His circle of concern is the situations or happenings that we have little or no control over and his circle of influence is the things in our lives that we can do something about.

I see this idea continually in coaching, as life is a combination of two seemingly opposing areas; the area of life we can do something about and the area of life we can do nothing about. The whole of our lives exist within these two areas. We can do something about our life circumstances, or we can do nothing about them. It's that simple. Although, each of us is unique, with our own life journeys and experiences, which contribute to how much ownership we do or don't have. There is no universal, concrete statistic on how much ownership we have in any given area of life. Factors vary from person to person and from time to time. Every week I coach people who are getting the issue of ownership out of balance, by either not taking ownership of the things they could or trying to take ownership of the things they can't. We are often just like kids playing netball and not understanding the zonal boundaries, because we don't know where the borders of our ownership are. We either think the area we own is much smaller than it is, or we consistently overstep the boundary line. To make matters trickier, our ownership doesn't have fixed, visible boundary fences. It has invisible borders that are constantly moving, depending upon the situation. It would be so much easier if it was a fixed boundary that never moved and was consistently the same, but it isn't. It's vital we empower ourselves and our clients to assess and reassess where the boundaries of ownership are, because when it comes to taking ownership, people tend to respond from four different mind-sets; *Moaning, Postponing, Controlling* and *Owning*. As a coach, understanding these mind-sets can be helpful, but it is never about labelling people with them. It is simply a case of enhancing our curiosity as we help our clients explore their responses to different situations and circumstances.

Moaning Mind-set

We are in a '*moaning mind-set*' when we are refusing to take ownership for an aspect of our life. What often makes us respond from this mind-set, is the belief the situation we are speaking about, is somebody or something else's fault. Moaning is a mind-set that believes the difficulties we are experiencing in our relationships, health, finances, career, social life or any other area, are nothing to do with us. We have convinced ourselves that this part of our life, is simply not our doing. Moaning causes us to deny ownership and replace it with a multitude of excuses and blame.

Steve had financial difficulties. He was about £70,000 in debt, which was a combination of loans and credit cards he'd run up over the previous decade. He was in a well-paid job earning over £75,000 a year; was single and had no children to support. When I asked about his debt, his reply was to tell me, *"It's the price of petrol, the government have absolutely screwed me with the tax on fuel. If it wasn't for them my finances would be fine and I would be able to live within my means".* His 'reason' for being in so much debt is laughable, it's so ridiculous to think the price of petrol is to blame. It is clearly just an excuse from someone in a '*moaning mind-set'* who is refusing to take ownership for his financial predicament. I discovered that Steve was in £70,000 worth of debt because somewhere along the line he spent £70,000 more than he made. Where does this '*moaning mind-set'* and refusal to take ownership leave Steve? It leaves him stuck. Whilst Steve continues to claim it is the government's fault, he is completely trapped. In making these excuses and blaming other people, Steve is giving away any chance he has to grow. Until Steve takes ownership for his financial situation, things cannot get any better. The truly sad part is it is clearly within Steve's ownership and capabilities to change this situation; he has the resources and the intelligence to make this better, but without taking ownership he renders himself incapacitated. Steve has given away his power to progress and he has handed control of his finances to an external, imaginary excuse.

It would be easy for us to pass judgment over Steve and condemn him for being so silly, but at times I can be just as guilty of taking up a '*moaning mind-set*'. It might not be about my finances, but rather my relationship, my health, my body or my career. I think we can all be like Steve, having areas of our life that are well within our ownership which we refuse to acknowledge and try to place outside of our control. The reason we make excuses, is quite simply because it's the easiest option. It's easier to pass the buck and blame someone or something, because then we don't have to admit it is our fault and we don't have to do anything. A '*moaning mind-set*' helps us avoid progressing, because if we have convinced ourselves we can't do anything about it, then we don't have to set out on the journey of growing. Plus, if we blame our upbringing, our teachers, our neighbours, our boss, our government, the weather, our families, our metabolism, our finances, our pets, our kids and our everything else, we believe we are no longer responsible for creating growth in our lives. We are masters of moaning. From the moment we could speak we started making excuses. As a little kid our excuses were quite obvious and blatant. "I didn't hear you", "I didn't do it", or "it was my sister/brother". We then became master crafters of excuses sometime in our teens. Our excuses and blames became cleverer and more convincing. By the time we become adults, making excuses and blaming has become so second nature to us, we barely even notice ourselves doing it. As our excuses and blames become more elaborate, they also become increasingly believable and subtle, which makes them sound more like the truth and harder to detect. That's what we are trying to achieve by our '*moaning mind-set*', that nobody will notice the excuse and we will get ourselves off the hook. Once our excuses and blame are this intricate, they are not only difficult for other people to spot, but they become difficult for us to notice ourselves. They start sounding very much like the truth to us and the more we say them, the more they sound like the truth, until even we can't tell an excuse from reality.

I used to have a great excuse for not starting my own business and staying in a job I knew I'd outgrown. I would tell people I had great business ideas, but I couldn't see them through and my amazing excuse got me off the hook with people every time. I used to say, "I can't start my own business because we want to start a family" which soon developed to "I can't start my own business because I've got a young family". I used to continue, "My job as a father is to provide security for my children. It's more important they have security, than I chase my dreams". Everyone who heard it thought how honourable it was for me to sacrifice my ambitions for the sake of my children. They would virtually applaud my selflessness. The truth is though, that it was simply a very clever, elaborate excuse. It was no more or less of an excuse than a blatant one, just nobler sounding, so that I didn't have to step out into the unknown and begin the journey of growth.

The price of a '*moaning mind-set'* is being trapped, unable to move forward in life and this is where coaching comes in. As a coach, it's imperative we help our clients explore their excuses and blames, go sightseeing around their mind-set to see if they are giving away their ownership of the situation, because unless our clients take the ownership available to them, they will not experience the growth and development they could.

Postponing Mind-set

Mary longs to find the right guy, fall in love, marry and have children. It's her unfulfilled ambition and something she has sought since her teenage years. Now in her mid-thirties, Mary is attractive, intelligent, authentic, funny and successful. She has had several great guys very interested in her over the years and yet she remains single. It doesn't really make sense to most people. What she wants so badly is to be married and has had numerous good opportunities to make this happen. Yet each time she lets it pass her by. It seems nonsensical until you realise that Mary is in a '*postponing mind-set'* around relationships. She is so scared of making a poor choice, of making a mistake and of marrying the *'wrong person'*, she is completely opting out of the decision-making process altogether. She isn't taking ownership for this part of her life and it's not because she wants to make excuses, it's because she is petrified of making a mistake. It is easier to just do nothing. A '*postponing mind-set'* comes about because of the fear of failure, the dread of disappointment and concern of getting it wrong.

'Postponing' is evident in us when we are stalling on making decisions and taking action in areas of our life that are well within our ownership. We might be staying in a job we hate because of the fear we may not get a better one; putting up with a poor relationship because we're so frightened to be alone or stalling on getting the qualifications we need because we may not pass the exams. A '*postponing mind-set'* creates a tendency to bury our head in the sand, to try and ignore the situation and pretend it's not happening. The big ploy is one of avoidance. Often '*postponing mind-sets'* also cause us to distract ourselves by being ridiculously busy, we have no time or energy to focus on taking ownership of what it is we really want.

Beth had a real flair for art. Her talent was unquestionable and her work brilliant. She excelled in art all the way through her education and on leaving university, still had ambitions to become a professional artist. She took a job working in a bank just to see her by until she could launch her career. That was 20 years ago and Beth can still be found behind the cashier's desk at that very same bank. Her art career has been on hold for over two decades. The reason is not Beth's talent or time, it is Beth's fear that no one will buy her work, she won't be good enough and she will be branded a failure. Despite numerous encouragements and offers of support from her friends and family, Beth has chosen a '*postponing mind-set'*. As the years have rolled by, postponing has become easier and easier and taking ownership, harder and harder for Beth.

'Postponing mind-sets' tend to convince us we are not really bothered, and the decision isn't that important. We will often say things like, "I don't really care if I get married or not", "I'm not ambitious, so changing careers is not important to me", "I don't need friends, so I don't care about my lack of social life". They are often statements intended to mask the true desires. The fear of not being able to grow, drives us to bury the truth from those around us and even from ourselves. Whilst we are in a '*postponing mind-set'*, we are robbing ourselves of the time we could have moving towards more of what we want. We are cheating ourselves of the growth we

could be experiencing and instead, living with the fear, discontent and dissatisfaction.

As a coach, it is again important to offer the opportunity for our clients to explore what is really going on for them in their '*postponing mind-set*', to offer the questions they may need to acknowledge and begin the work of growth.

Controlling Mind-set

People have been wrestling for control since the dawn of humankind. We seem to have an inbuilt desire to feel as though we are in complete control of all areas of our lives. Yet this idea of complete control is a myth. There are huge parts of our lives we are simply not in control of and never will be. Our own mortality should be enough to emphasise this to us. Every time we get in a car we take the risk of having an accident because we are not in control of other road user's actions, every conversation we engage in we are not in control of the words the other speaks and every time we plan a day trip we have no control of the weather. There is a seemingly endless list of events we are not in control of and areas where we have no say over the outcome or situation. '*Controlling*' is a mind-set that struggles to accept the events that are beyond the boundaries of our ownership. There is a striving to control areas of life that were never meant to be controlled and to exert ownership in aspects of life that cannot ever be owned. Being like this creates a plethora of worry about what events might happen, stress about events that are happening and even anger about the lack of control. A '*controlling mind-set*' lives in fear of the world outside our ownership, struggling to cope with the thought of having this big area of life, we can do absolutely nothing about.

I only really became conscious of my '*controlling mind-set*' when my first child was born. I had absolutely no idea what to expect during the birth of a child. Like the beginning of a romantic novel, it was Christmas night when our beautiful baby girl arrived, but this idyllic staging did nothing to mask the trauma of the birth. There were complications and I vividly remember listening through a monitor to the slowing of our baby's heartbeat, as each contraction hit. I also recall the moment where a room full of medical professionals held their breath, as the sound of deafening silence poured out of the monitor's speakers and I realised that our baby's heart had stopped beating. I have no idea how long her heart beat paused, but at that time it was the longest moment of my life. The thought of losing our baby, before we had even held her was horrifying. I only endured this fear momentarily, not the unbearable pain of losing a child that some of my friends have suffered. The doctors did their work and my daughter entered this world battered and bruised but healthy, just before midnight on Christmas Day. This experience, although brief, enhanced my awareness of how much I was striving to control. Later that night, it really dawned on me, as I finished praying the most ludicrous prayer I have ever prayed. In the early hours of Boxing Day morning, I was ordered home to sleep by the hospital night staff. As I drove away leaving my wife and our baby in the ward, I prayed. It went something like this, "God, please keep my baby alive and her heart beating until I return in the morning, when I can watch over her". It was almost as if I was saying to God, "Don't worry, Big Guy, if you can do the night shift, when I get back in the morning I'll take over. I know that you are meant to be the creator and sustainer of all life, but I'll take on that role once I've had some sleep". Seriously! Who did I think I was? A higher power who had dominion over life and death? A medical professional with great knowledge of human health? No, I was just me, a new father in his twenties, who had absolutely no control over the labour, the birth or whether my baby lived or died that night. It was an event I could do nothing about and it hit me, that up until that point, I had subtly been exhibiting a *'controlling mind-set'* towards a number of events in my life, that were in fact uncontrollable. Three months after my daughter was born, my dad had a heart-attack and it reminded me again, that I'm not in control.

I see this similar *'controlling mind-set'* in many people, in various walks of life. The mother controlling the lives of her fully-grown children, the boss controlling every decision his staff make, the husband controlling his wife, the wife controlling her husband, the ageing woman controlling her wrinkles and the teenagers controlling their body shapes. The list is endless. There are certain things in life that are just not meant to be controlled and are impossible to take ownership over. A '*controlling mind-set*' gives the illusion of control, but it can also mean the fun and spontaneity are suffocated out of life. Sometimes the unexpected, the unpredictable, the unknown and the random events that happen to us provide us with the most exciting, funny and memorable moments of our lives. Spontaneous, random events over which we have no control, can bring much colour to our existence.

At a wedding in snow covered Canada, just north of Vancouver, the bride and groom chose to have their ceremony outside a lodge, by the edge of a frozen lake. It was a spectacular setting, with mountains and fir trees covered in pure white snow, like a scene from the Land of Narnia. As the couple began to say their vows to each other, there was a murmur from the small congregation assembled, as one by one they noticed a beautiful, wild, black bear making his way across the lake, just yards from the ceremony. From my viewpoint, the bear stood for a moment as if directly between the bride and groom, looked over to see what was happening and slowly moved along his way. It was the first time I had ever seen a bear in the wild and there couldn't have been a more beautiful moment. This couple had meticulously planned their wedding, they had organised every last detail and prepared for almost any eventuality and yet it was an unpredictable event that stole the show. All that planning, organising and controlling was upstaged by a blissfully unaware bear. It is an event to be cherished and an event that added more colour, wonder and memorability to that day than anything that could have been controlled.

Events will happen, it's part of life. As a coach I simply try to assist my clients to work through any '*controlling mind-sets*' they have, by helping them to find acceptance in the events of life and take ownership for their responses, as best they can.

Owning Mind-set

The '*owning mind-set*' happens when we take real and complete ownership for everything that is within our control, whilst being able to accept and respond to the situations that occur outside of our ownership. In an '*owning mind-set*' we are brave enough to take ownership of our situation, humble enough to accept the events outside our control, secure enough to hold up our hand to our own mistakes, whilst conscious enough to choose our responses. Taking ownership is not about being in control of everything, it is about finding that place of balance between what is and isn't within our ownership. This is not a new idea, far from it. It is a revamped ancient truth that I have been able to relearn. The Serenity Prayer by Reinhold Niebuhr sums up exactly what an '*owning mind-set*' is.

God grant me the serenity to accept the things I cannot change;
courage to change the things I can; and wisdom to know the difference.

Wisdom to know the difference is the one thing that truly creates an '*owning mind-set*'. We don't make excuses, procrastinate or try to control the things we can't change. We know exactly where the boundary lines are. We also recognise when these boundaries naturally shift and accept this movement as part of life. This is the reason it is vital to continually reassess with clients, where ownership is and how they best accept events outside their control, whilst taking ownership for their responses. I don't speak about acceptance and response lightly, because sometimes it can be the hardest thing in the world to achieve, yet there are people I have encountered who seem to have found incredible levels of acceptance and response.

I heard Darren speak publicly about the sudden death of his son. It was one of the most profound moments of my life. I listened as he explained his pain, anger and grief at his loss. I hung on his every word as he described the questions he asked of the doctors, himself and God. I was overwhelmed by the peace and acceptance he had managed to find in his heart when the answers never came. With empathetic tears in my eyes, I heard him describe how he now travels around the country offering support to parents facing similar events in their lives. There is no reason I could hear for the death of his son, it was just a terribly, terribly sad event. However, this man has found an incredible reply, some level of acceptance and response that I felt more in his presence than in any of the words he spoke.

Sarah had a difficult child-hood to say the least. She was raised by her mother who neglected her in many ways. She mistreated Sarah so badly it resulted in her eyesight deteriorating so severely in her teenage years, that Sarah was registered blind. She had a problem with her eyes that could have been easily treated. Although her mum knew about this, she didn't take Sarah to her hospital appointments, so the Doctors weren't able to treat her, until it was too late. Due to her mum's neglect, Sarah was taken into care as a teenager and lived with a foster family. She eventually lost her eyesight at the age of 16. If ever someone had a reason for a *'moaning mind-set'*, it was

Sarah. She could have blamed her mum, her blindness, the care system and a thousand other things. She could also have decided to have a *'controlling mind-set'* to protect herself and try to ensure events outside of her control, never hurt her again. What Sarah did decide to do was to adopt an *'owning mind-set'* to her past. She accepted the events that had happen to her and she decided to respond in the best way possible. I asked her once how she felt towards her mum, she responded with three simple but powerful words... *"I forgive her"*. Sarah knew she could blame her past, but she also knew if she took ownership of her life, she could create a great future for herself. Sarah is now a happily married woman, a motivational speaker and an International Athlete.

Coaching Ownership

We will exhibit each of these mind-sets in differing areas of life and our clients will do the same. As a coach, we will witness clients dance between each mind-set as the conversation moves and flows. It is not our job as the coach, to get our clients to adopt an owning mind-set, it is simply to offer them the chance to explore their mind-sets and trust, as always, that as they do so they will find their own way forward. Listening for and recognising these mind-sets, both in ourselves and our clients, empowers our curiosity to ask more helpful questions and aids our client's internal growth in the way they see and think about themselves. Ultimately growth cannot happen without ownership and it is only in enabling our clients to explore their own version of ownership that development occurs.

Chapter 7

Acceptance – Embracing all our names

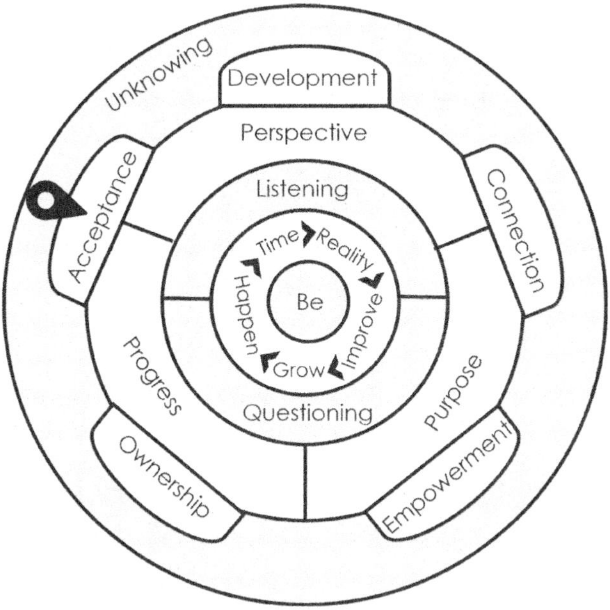

"The most terrifying thing is to accept oneself completely."

Carl Jung

Changing Names

I changed my name once. We were on a family holiday and I was 8 years old. I can't remember exactly where, but it was a campsite nestling in the rolling hills of England. Like all decent campsites, it had a play area in the middle where the children would congregate and make friends with other kids, sporting a variety of strange and mysterious accents. It was there, with my brother, about ten minutes after we had arrived that the other kids started to introduce themselves. As they did, I immediately had an overwhelming sense of inferiority. All these kids had really "exciting" names. They might not be exciting now, but back in the 1980's their names were amazing. The first boy to speak opened with "Hi, my name's Luke", which in my 8-year-old mind made him a Jedi Knight. Luke's friend was called Daniel, just like the Karate Kid and his brother was called Michael, the name of Knight Rider, the guy with the smartest car on television. Now this wouldn't have been a problem if my name wasn't John, but at the time nobody exciting was called John. The only person on television I could think about called John; was John Craven, the presenter of Newsround, which is possibly the most sensible kids TV show ever made. So, as an 8-year-old, stood in a campsite play area, in the middle of I-don't-know-where, I decided in an instant to change my name. John just wasn't going to 'cut the mustard' amongst this plethora of the most exciting names on the planet. I took it upon myself to tell Luke, Daniel and Michael that everyone back home just called me "Face". Face! That was me, sharing a name with the best-looking member of the A-Team. Me, a bright ginger-haired kid, covered in immeasurable freckles from head to toe, called "Face". The unbelievable part to this story is that they accepted it without query. "Hi Face, great to meet you. What football team do you support?" came Luke's response. My brother looked at me; and I looked back, hoping beyond hope he wouldn't reveal the truth. To my relief he seemed to like the idea of this name changing and introduced himself as "Hawke" and for a few days, Face and Hawke played confidently in the knowledge that our names were as exciting as any other kids on the site.

The Power of Names

Changing my name as an 8-year-old meant I had unwittingly stumbled upon something that I thought was bringing improvement to my life. When I was Face, I was more exciting, I strutted a bit more when I walked, I took the lead over older kids and I spoke with more certainty, but what was truly happening was perhaps not really that helpful at all. I had rejected the name John for myself during that week, because I thought of it as boring and I wanted to be Face, because Face was exciting. I didn't realise it at the time, but as an 8-year-old, I inadvertently discovered there is something powerful in the names we call ourselves and yet something even more forceful in the names we try to reject.

I remember vividly being 6 years old, in the playground at school, when I heard it said for the first time. My friend Nick shouted it at a girl who had just called him 'Speccy Four Eyes'. "Sticks and stones will break my bones, but names will never hurt me". I liked it at the time, I remember thinking it was clever and I was proud of Nick's retort in my own 6-year-old kind of way. Having said that, it is quite possibly the biggest lie I've ever heard, because names can hurt us more subtly than we even know. In fact, names hold the potential to completely dictate and dominate our lives.

The power that names hold isn't a modern phenomenon; civilisations throughout history have known this. In many ancient cultures names held meanings. Children were given a name which reflected their personalities, position or the hope of a future accomplishment. In many Native American tribes, names were not even fixed, but changed numerous times throughout a person's lifetime. Names really do affect us. They impact the way we feel, the things we do and the choices we make. As children we were called many names, ranging from playground taunts, to pet names given to us by our parents. We will have heard all kinds of differing names describing who we are from our peers, siblings, teachers, family, neighbours, friends and even ourselves. Although we might not have known it, these names became the names we started to call ourselves. They became our perspective of ourselves. Even after everybody else may have stopped referring to us by them, we perhaps continued to silently and even sometimes unconsciously, define ourselves by these names.

Not the Whole Story

I love the Mr Men and Little Miss characters. They are such a beautifully simple concept. My children have the whole collection of Mr Men books, the ones that if you put them in the right order on your shelf you can see the full Mr Men logo written on their side. One night, when my eldest two kids were small I asked them which Mr Men book they would like me to read before bedtime and they both agreed (which is unusual in itself) on Mr Happy. Before I opened the book, I asked what they thought might happen in the story. They both looked at me as if I had asked the most ridiculous of questions. At 3 and 4 years of age, they declared in unison and with a hint of child-like sarcasm, "I think he will be really HAPPY!" It was an obvious answer; of course, Mr Happy would be happy, what else could he be? Here lies the beauty of the Mr Men, they always behave in the way their name suggests; Mr Happy is always happy and Mr Grumpy is always grumpy, Little Miss Late is always late, and Mr Bump is always bumping into things. It's the predictable genius of the whole Mr Men and Little Miss cast, they behave exactly as their name suggests. It's so obvious, but so brilliant. The perspective they hold of themselves on the inside, utterly dictates the way in which they behave on the outside.

Yet for us, at our purest state, we are the opposite of Mr Men and Little Miss, because as human beings we don't just have one name or one way of being. We are layer after layer of intricacy and complexity, which means we hold within ourselves such potential for an almighty plethora of names and ways of being, that we are too multifaceted to even fathom. Yet, because of our desire to accept some names for ourselves and reject others, we have reduced ourselves to a handful of dominate names, that make us at times, more like Mr Men than humans. These dominant names we call ourselves become the blueprint for who we think we are and how we believe we should behave. Yet, whatever names we call ourselves are never the whole story, because we have within us such a vast range of capabilities. The difference between us and Mr Men is that they have one name and we have infinite names. They have one persuasion and we have countless. I have both quietness and loudness within me, I have confidence and doubt, I have intelligence and stupidity and the whole range in between. The danger is not so much in the names we and our clients call ourselves; it is more that some of our names have begun to dominate our lives. We have labelled ourselves with great big name badges, that dominate our understanding of ourselves and in doing so have hemmed ourselves in and stunted our growth. It happens to us through our conditioning. We can be with certain names and characteristics for ourselves, yet we have whole other parts of ourselves we try to shut down and keep quiet, because for some reason we find them unacceptable. At 8-years-old on that campsite, John, was simply unacceptable, it was too boring, too plain and I didn't want to show John to the world; I wanted Face, because Face was cool and exciting. By embracing *exciting* and rejecting *boring*, I believed I was creating positivity in my life, but what I was really doing was denying a really useful part of my self, because sometimes as strange as it might sound at first, I will need boring, just as much as I will need exciting.

By having these dominate names for ourselves, we run the risk of becoming one dimensional, just like Mr Men. Whatever name we call ourselves, is exactly how we will behave. It would be so strange to open a Mr Men book that began, "Today Mr Messy was being very tidy" or a Little Miss book that read "Little Miss Naughty was being extremely well behaved". It just doesn't fit, it wouldn't seem right. It's impossible for Mr Men to go against their names and when we have dominant names it is difficult for us, as people to go against them too. We will, unwittingly make our lives align with the names we call ourselves. If we only call ourselves *shy,* no matter how many confidence building courses we go on, our behaviour will always at some point return to our name. If we call ourselves *fat,* no matter how many diets we start, we will faithfully wander back each time to align our body with this name. If we are *failure,* no matter how many snippets of success we experience, we will consistently spring back to the feeling our name dictates. If we only call ourselves *intelligent,* when we don't understand something, we will cover it up. If our dominant name is *brave,* when we experience fear, we will feel shame.

Names We've Adopted

Unwittingly we will have spent our whole lives being given and adopting names by a whole host of people. You might have been called all sorts of names like good, bad, clumsy, pretty, ugly, helpful, useless, brave, weak, clever, thick, fat, skinny and an endless list of others.

What we have learnt through our lives, is that some of these names for ourselves are acceptable to us and to those around us, and some of these names are not. We adopt the acceptable ones and try and keep the unacceptable ones down. We might imagine that it is all the positive, uplifting names we adopt and the shameful, darker ones we keep down, but that is not always the case. We often simply adopt the names that others around us accept the most, regardless of whether they sound good or bad.

One of the names I was given as a child was '*butterfingers*'. I can't remember how many times I was called this, it might only have been a few but it was a name that stuck with me. It was a name I adopted for myself and it was a name I believed whole heartedly. I'm unsure which came first, the name or the behaviour? Did I drop things all the time? Was I clumsy with my hands? Is that why I was labelled '*butterfingers*'? Or did I just believe it and therefore act clumsy because I was living up to the name? Having this name certainly affected the way I behaved. I believed I was useless with my hands, so I would either deliberately avoid doing handy jobs, or my confidence was so low, I would end up dropping things, making mistakes and reinforcing the belief I was '*butterfingers*'. I totally lived up to the name. I carried this name into my adulthood and right up to my mid-twenties; I hadn't ever even considered it or begun to entertain the idea of alternatives. In my mind, '*butterfingers*' was just the way I was and it described the whole of me. At the age of 27, I had an opportunity to buy a derelict terrace house for a cheap price, but the only way it could be a good investment would be to do most of the repair work myself. Being '*butterfingers*' I would never even have looked at a house like that, but a very persuasive and good friend of mine advised me to purchase it. I rebuffed him in no uncertain terms and explained how ridiculous it was, I was '*butterfingers*', there was no way I could restore a derelict house. I couldn't even hold a screw driver, I'd never put shelves up and the only thing remotely handy I had done was make a dodgy wooden spatula in woodwork class at school. "I am '*butterfingers*'", I told him. My friend's reply was surprising, "What do you mean you're '*butterfingers*'? Whoever told you that? You've got great hand to eye coordination, you're creative, hard-working and if I show you a couple of things, you'll definitely be able to do this." I argued with him. I did not give up my label of *'butterfingers'* easily, because it was all I had. However, it was the first time I had even begun to question it and through this questioning I discovered the name was not the whole story. There was much more to me than just butterfingers. I bought the house and over 6 months renovated it, from top to bottom. The housing market exploded in the meantime and we eventually sold the house two and a half years later for almost three times as much as it had cost us. Imagine what I may have lost if I'd never explored that name and what other possibilities lay within me. I don't mean financially, that was never the real success, I mean the loss of skills, adventure and accomplishment. In renovating that house, I discovered so much about myself, who I am and what I am really capable of. There is a part of me that is '*butterfingers*', but another part that is *"do it yourself savvy"* and everything in between. It is a period of my life I look back on with enormous satisfaction. I could have missed out on the experience and development, purely because I had adopted a name for myself that wasn't the whole story.

Names We Think We Should Be

We have numerous dominant names we think we "should" be. We should be richer, slimmer, happier, cleverer, better, braver, stronger. Most of these names have been born out of our habit of comparing. We have looked at other people and compared ourselves, which creates names in us we believe we "should" be. Sometimes this comparing might have been done for us, by the others in our life. Our parents may have compared us to our siblings, or our teachers compared us to our classmates. Sometimes it is simply us that does all the comparing. Our tendency for this has perhaps been increased further by our exposure to the media and world of celebrity. Due to the saturation of the commercial world around us, we even unwittingly compare ourselves with airbrushed, P.R. manipulated, perfect versions of people who don't even exist in real life. However, perhaps the most damaging of all our comparisons and the root of much of our "should be" names, stems from our insistence to compare ourselves with some idealistic, fantasy version of ourselves. Carl Rogers talked about our 'Ideal Self', this perfect version of us that lives only in our imagination and does nothing other than give us the sense of falling short of this flawless person, that we 'should' be. Our "should be" names quite simply make us feel inadequate. They make us strive and struggle to be someone we are not; to live up to an image of ourselves that is not the real us. Our "should be" names drive us to project false images and they keep us from being able to fully accept ourselves, just as we are. We can create a public face to display to others in the hope they will buy into this smokescreen. Somehow, it gives us a sense we are living up to the names we should be and yet, all it is doing is robbing us of the time and energy we could be putting into accepting and developing our real selves.

Susan came for coaching because something had dawned on her. A few weeks previous she was frustrated and exhausted. She was two years into her degree course and hating every minute of it. She was studying to be an accountant even though she loathed working with numbers and it wasn't something she was even particularly adept at. Whilst speaking with a close friend one night about her frustrations, she had a revelation. She didn't want to be an accountant at all and she never had done. Her whole reason for choosing this degree was because she "should be" as successful as her half-sister. In that moment, when she heard those words in her mind, she realised for the first time the direction of her whole life was being driven by her father's comparisons of her to her half-sister. She decided to come for coaching and figure out who she really was and what she really wanted.

My ears prick up when the people I work with use the word 'should' in a description of themselves. It's almost a sure sign they are not speaking from their real self, but from some sense of obligation. I find myself often simply reflecting the word back at them as a question, 'should?', with the intention of helping them explore who else they are, rather than what they think they should be .

Names We're Sure We're Not

There is a two-word phrase I hear in coaching on a regular basis, it goes like this, *"I'm not."* What then follows, is a declaration of something my client believes they are not. e.g. *"a risk taker, adventurous, a bitch, a gossip, weak, very open, scared, someone who talks about my feelings, emotional, confrontational, confident etc."*

My friend Robbie recounted to me his experience of his first day at high school. He was nervous about making new friends, as many 11-year-olds would be. At the first break-time of the day, Robbie was stood in his classroom when another boy from a different class walked in. This boy had been at Primary School with one of the other boys in Robbie's class and had come to see how his pal was getting on. He asked his friend, *"Hey, what are the people like in your new class?"* His friend then took it upon himself to give a full run down of each person in the class. He looked at each person one by one, pointed at them and said, *"he's alright", "she's nice", "I like him".* When he got to Robbie, he pointed at him and simply said, *"He's not good at talking to people"*. Twenty-five years later, I could still hear the pain in Robbie's voice when he told me this story. He tried to laugh it off, but he couldn't mask it. I asked him if he still thought of himself this way and whether he ever referred to himself as *"not good at talking to people"*. He told me he would often repeat this statement when he described himself. He often let people know that *"I'm not good at talking to people"* and this *"I'm not"* name still haunted him whenever he was meeting new people. It dominated him and in particular, when Robbie went off to university it had a huge impact. In his four years there, he would turn down invites to parties, never respond when a girl showed an interest in him, become panic stricken at the thought of presentations and mumble his words whenever he met friends of friends. All this because of the idea that *"I'm not good at talking to people"* spoken by an 11-year-old, who didn't even really know him and even if he did, was only telling one side of a story. There is some truth that in certain situations Robbie isn't good at talking to people, yet he is also one of the most articulate, interesting and expressive people I've ever met. It is in the wholeness of Robbie that the wonder of who he is, is found, not just in one or other of the names he could call himself, but in all of them.

I also used to have a big list of names that I thought I wasn't and they all started with *"I'm not the kind of person who could... run a business, write a book, go on rollercoasters, show emotion, be ambitious, make a real difference, give up a steady income, take risks."* Each of these statements created an "I'm not" in me, that until I was able to notice and work with, they defined and limited my life. Somewhere in our upbringing we decided there are things we're definitely not. Our list of who we're "not" will be varied and yet all of our "I'm Not Names" have one thing in common. They keep us down, because they are only one side of the story. They protect us from other parts of ourselves that perhaps we can't be with, but they also rob us of tapping into all those other names we may have, that are useful and have their part to play in the fullness of who we are. As a coach it offers us the opportunity to help our clients explore these perspectives and names of who they are not, from a different angle, perhaps enabling them to see the bigger picture of the range of names they truly have within them.

Names we have Rejected

Throughout our life, we will have spent a huge amount of time rejecting and dismissing names that people have tried to give us; names that may be helpful in giving us a broader perspective of ourselves. I rejected countless names for myself, one of these being "Creative". In my early adulthood, people would tell me I was a creative thinker, that I had an ability to see things from a fresh perspective and I could think outside of the proverbial box. I would reject this name of creative out of hand. I refused this name for myself. Even though it is a name that could help bring vibrancy to my life, I would just not accept it. I couldn't adopt it as a name for myself. The reason was, it seemed to conflict with a name that I already had. That name was *"no imagination".* I was certain that I had no imagination and therefore that meant I couldn't possibly be *"creative".* Those two names, for me, were polar-opposites of each other. Every time I heard someone call me creative, I would assume they were being kind, mistaken or just simply lying, because I knew that really, I was '*no-imagination'*. My certainty over this name of '*no-imagination'* was an after effect of my childhood. When I was a child, I was never interested in playing with action figures and making up stories about their adventures. I preferred to run around and play sports. I had no time for creating make-believe tales. My parents misinterpreted my desire of not playing with figures, as me suffering from a lack of imagination. So, I heard this phrase "he's got no imagination" repeatedly. I heard this statement about myself from my parents, my grandparents and my siblings. As a child I never questioned this name. I just simply accepted and adopted the fact that I had '*no-imagination'.* Twenty years later I started to notice people repeatedly referring to me as "creative" and it just didn't fit. No wonder I rejected it, no wonder when someone spoke the words "you are so creative" I would shove them aside as quickly as I could. It finally dawned on me one day at work when my boss appeared at the side of my desk and said to me, *"I need your help, you're so creative and I need some creativity right now"*. The penny dropped. I started to ask how can I be creative when I've got no imagination? Everyone seems to be telling me that I'm creative and there's only me (and distant childhood memories) telling me that I'm 'no-imagination'. Yet it isn't about one being right and the other being wrong, it's that I have all the capability to range from no imagination in one circumstance, to creative in another. They both live within me, it's just that for years I couldn't hear or feel anything at the other end of the spectrum. This is the danger with names, that one dominates and we believe it is the totality of who we are. Yet, there is so much more within us to discover, if only we are given the environment in which to explore.

I witness people rejecting names for themselves, almost on a daily basis. I see people batting away compliments before they even have chance to land in their ears. I notice friends, family and colleagues wrestling to take on board even the smallest of positive praise, because it simply doesn't fit with the list of names they already call themselves. We need to listen (really listen) to the alternative names that are there for us.

One of the reasons we instantly reject names, is because we have developed the habit of using invisible earplugs and invisible ping pong bats. Denise consistently wears her invisible ear plugs. As soon as anyone so much as attempts to compliment her, to give her a positive comment, she puts in her invisible ear plugs and waits until it is safe to take them out again. She is not rude or dismissive of the person complimenting her; she just sits there blankly with her invisible ear plugs in, not able to really hear a word they are saying. It's just like a child, who doesn't want to hear something, so places their fingers in their ears and sings loudly so they cannot hear a word being said. Denise and her invisible ear plugs are just a grown up, politer version of this. Mike doesn't have invisible ear plugs; instead he has an invisible ping pong bat. Mike is really kind, helpful and generous. He is one of life's good guys. But as soon as a compliment or a word of thanks is fired in his direction, his hands come up as if he's holding a ping pong bat and he knocks away the compliment, before it has had time to land in his ears and mind. He hears the positive praise but bats it away before it has chance to really sink in. He follows that up with words such as "It was nothing", "No problem", "It was easy", "It's fine, no big deal". The result in this batting away is it stops Mike from ever truly accepting a compliment and ultimately hearing alternative names for himself.

Accepting All Our Names

In the end it boils down to our ability to accept the whole of ourselves and not just the names, we and others find acceptable. It is about seeing that the names we have tried to keep down, have a part to play in our lives. At times my *faithfulness* is very helpful, it keeps relationships and friendships in my life on track, yet at other times *faithfulness* can be a big hindrance. It can keep me in relationships and friendships, that are no longer healthy and way past their best before date. It is *unfaithfulness* I need more of. At times being *strong* is absolutely what I need in life, but not always, because sometimes I need *weakness.* Other times being *non-judgemental* is the most helpful part of me, but then on occasions the *judgemental* me keeps me safe. We have become so transfixed on accepting a few dominant names for ourselves that we have lost so much of who we fully are. It is only in our complete and utter acceptance of the whole of us, of every name we have, our whole story and our whole self that we find the foundation to grow.

By not being able to accept the whole of us, with all our names and capabilities, we are closing parts of ourselves down and limiting ourselves. To be fully living, we need all of ourselves, the whole lot, with every name and characteristic we have. What stops us from being able to accept ourselves in our entirety, is because of our incessant need to label things as good and bad, as positive and negative. If we see *strong* as a positive and *weak* as a negative, we may try to reject and deny our weakness. If we see *confidence* as good and *insecurity* as bad, we will hide our *insecurity* away. But there is no universal positive or negative, good or bad, because it depends on each circumstance and situation. In some settings I need my *strong* self, but in others I need *weakness*. In some affairs *confidence* would be helpful, but in others it would be unhelpful, and *insecurity* would be of more use. There is no part of us, no name that is better than any other. They all have the potential to be helpful or unhelpful, positive or negative from circumstance to circumstance. Once we truly believe this, then we can open the doors to accept all our names and the whole of us, without shame or fear. All of who we are has a part to play and the first step to tapping into our whole self is being able to accept and make peace with the whole story of who we are.

Coaching Names

It is important to work with our clients' names. Notice them, be curious about them and at times challenge them. We need to listen for our clients' dominant names and help them to explore these names. Empowering them to look at the full range of who they are, not just the dominant names they are living up to. When I think I may have heard a client give themselves a name, I often reflect it back to them and offer the opportunity to explore other perspectives. If we are aware of the names they call themselves, we will start to notice the times they speak them out. If we are truly listening, we will hear their names. As a coach this helps us in understanding our clients and truly seeing their map of themselves. It gives us greater scope for asking better questions about these names. In day to day conversations, people's names for themselves often pass by without even acknowledgement. Someone refers to themselves as 'stupid', 'clever' or 'lazy' and their companions do nothing other than accept these names without thought and continue the conversation. What happens to the speaker though, is this passive response from the listeners is interpreted as agreement or collusion, that the name they have spoken is true. The speaker leaves that interaction more certain than ever before that all they are is 'stupid', 'clever' or 'lazy' and the rest of the world agrees too. Every time we speak out a name and it isn't acknowledged or heard, this acts as confirmation to us that our name is true, an irrefutable fact. We can't let our clients' names pass by like a bus we forgot to put out a hand to, or a taxi we didn't hail in time. We must be curious about their names, ask questions, help them explore, look at alternatives and see themselves as a whole person. They are full of wondrous amounts of potential. They possess names that span the full range of who they are, from their darkest depths to their highest heights.

Chapter 8

The Positions: More than A to B

"Not all those who wander are lost."

J.R.R. Tolkien, The Fellowship of the Ring

Coaching is Dangerous

"I don't want coaching because coaching is dangerous!"

Those were the words a bright, energetic, Business Manager, in her early forties told Dan, one of our coaches, who she had just met at a business networking event.

She continued, "I don't want coaching because the last time I had coaching, I left a job I really loved."

After a decade immersed in the coaching industry, I agree. The kind of coaching that simply charts a path for people from A to B, that forces people down paths they don't want to walk, that pushes people towards external goals they haven't fully considered and drives people forward before they are ready for the journey, is dangerous. I've seen the danger of coaching in all kinds of places. From 'coaches' making outrageous claims and promises that their programme or system is the answer to all our hopes and prayers, to vulnerable people being exploited at mass personal development gatherings by guru 'coaches', and in the case of the lady that Dan met, I've seen danger in 'coaches' driving their clients towards goals they don't even truly want. Based on my own experiences, I'd sadly have to agree, this version of coaching is dangerous because it is so obsessed with the destination it neglects the process. If this is all coaching has to offer, then I personally wouldn't touch it. Gloomily, I could tell story after story of things being wrapped up as ‘coaching’, that are potentially dangerous.

But this isn’t really coaching, it’s a wolf in sheep’s clothing, a hybrid of coaching masquerading as the real deal.

Whatever Dan’s lady experienced was obviously called ‘coaching’, but it wasn’t really because true coaching is not that kind of dangerous. It doesn’t exploit, drive or promise anything to people. It doesn’t command, persuade or push and if it does, then it’s not really coaching, it’s something else altogether.

One Dimensional Coaching

When I first started coaching, all the advice I ever received was that I needed to niche my coaching. I needed to let people know exactly who it was that I wanted to work with. I needed to be a business coach, a young people’s coach, a relationship coach or a confidence coach. From a marketing point of view that is perhaps, very true. It makes perfect sense to niche, so people know what circumstances or situations we coach. People can clearly see whether their circumstances fit with us as a coach. The problem with that though, is I don’t coach circumstances and situations. I’m not really interested in only circumstances changing, because circumstances are a temporary state. I’m interested in people growing, because if people grow, their circumstances and situations look after themselves. I coach people, I coach whole human beings, their circumstances and situations come into it because it's part of their experience but ultimately, it's about them developing themselves from the inside out. It doesn't matter to me what their circumstances are because I coach who they are, not what they do. This has left me with no definable niche other than people. The niche stuff is just a marketing thing, a business tool. I love people and they are my niche, humans of all kinds in all situations. I also don't coach parts of people, I coach the whole person. We may find ourselves talking about a part of their life, but what is always going on is the idea of how that impacts them as a whole person.

Traditionally coaching has been very one dimensional. It has helped people to make progress in specific areas of life, to create movement from A to B. It has been used in many instances to great effect as a way to create momentum and forward motion in people's circumstances. This type of coaching is what I would refer to as *progress coaching*. It is simply focused on the external progress a client is making, like the career promotion they are after, the relationship they wish to improve or the physical fitness they want to gain. Although I believe this is an important part of coaching, it is certainly not the totality of it. There is so much more to coaching than just movement from point A to point B. There is real worth to be found in *progress coaching,* but it is severely lacking if used solely in isolation. There are two other vital ingredients that must be in the mix of coaching and human growth. Yet, they are very often overlooked by the coaches who are desperate for their clients to make some tangible progress. If we are to coach the whole person, it is vital we empower our clients to explore both their perspectives and purposes, before we even begin the process of progress coaching. If we set off with our clients towards progress without first having looked with them at their perspectives and purposes, we could quite feasibly coach them down a path they don't really want to be without them even knowing.

Perspective coaching is about exploring the way a client sees themselves, others and the world around them. It's the glasses through which they are looking at life.

Purpose coaching is about people understanding what is driving and motivating them in a certain direction or behaviour.

Neither *perspective* or *purpose coaching* necessarily take our clients anywhere on the outside, but they do enable them to explore and discover what is really happening for them on the inside. Given the opportunity to do this often dramatically changes the direction of travel in their life.

Metaphorically, I think of my clients as being on the journey of growth and if this journey was taking place physically it would be as though their *purpose* is the reason for the journey, their *perspective* is looking at what is around them from new and different angles and their *progress* is the steps they are taking to move along their path. In another way, *purpose coaching* is working with someone's heart, *perspective coaching* is working with their eyes and *progress coaching* is working with their feet.

Perspective Coaching

Humans don't just experience the world, we interpret it! We filter it all through our map of the world and depending on that map, we can see the same world in very different ways, as though we are looking at the same thing but through different coloured glasses.

On 13th October 1972 a Uruguayan Air Force flight carrying 45 people, including a young rugby team and their entourage, was flying across the Andes when it ran into difficulty and crashed into some of the most remote and inhospitable terrain on earth. More than a quarter of the passengers died during the crash itself and many more died from their injuries or the freezing conditions in the first few days after the disaster. As if that wasn't enough, a further eight of the crash survivors were killed by an avalanche that without warning ploughed through their stricken wreck site. Eventually, 2 months and 10 days after the crash just 16 people were rescued from the mountain. However, this was no ordinary rescue by a hi-tech team of mountain experts. In fact, 2 months after the crash, through a crackling radio pulled from the wreckage, the survivors learnt the search for them had been called off. They were faced with a stark choice. A choice to sit it out in the hope somehow, somebody would stumble upon them, or audaciously, to find a way to climb out of the Andes and get help. Nando Parrado, a 22-year-old member of the rugby team and his companion Robert Canessa who at the time was still a teenager, decided to set out on the near impossible challenge of finding a way out of the longest continental mountain range in the world with little rations, no climbing gear and unsuitable clothing. Near the beginning of their journey is where the pivotal moment in their survival occurs. There is a scene in “Alive” (the film adaptation of the story) where Nando and Canessa climb a mountain peak, Canessa tires and rests just a few hundred yards from the summit. Nando presses on and when he reaches the top what he sees fills him with such excitement that he shouts for Canessa to come and see. Canessa, with new found energy, continues his climb in the hope he will see salvation and the green valleys of Chile. However, as Canessa arrives at the summit he slumps to his knees in utter despondence at the view that greets him, *"Mountains, nothing but mountains! We've had it, we've completely had it"*, he wails.

Nando however, sees a different view, because his focus is not the mountains themselves, but something else. *"No we haven't. Between these mountains somewhere there's a green valley. See these mountains over here, there's no snow on them."*

Canessa still reeling from his disappointment snaps back, *"Those mountains must be 50 miles away, you think you can walk 50 miles?"*

With great composure and assurance, Nando replies, *"If we have to, we will... you see there, where the sun's going to set. That way is west and to the west are the green valleys of Chile."*

It's the same view, but two different perspectives. One of these perspectives brought hope and the other despair. One brought motivation and the other despondence.

From Canessa's perspective, there were too many mountains in the way. The mountains were enormous and unassailable, so he was ready to give up, lay down and die right there, and who could have blamed him? He had already given so much in his fight for survival. However, from

Nando's perspective it was the mountains that gave him hope. The mountains weren't obstacles in his way; they were the place he was trying to reach. The mountains without snow on their peaks were his destination and seeing that gave him the motivation and the strength to find a way to achieve the impossible. Canessa was looking at what was wrong whilst Nando was focussed at what was right. Ten days after standing on that mountain peak Nando and Canessa were walking through the green valleys of Chile towards their and their companions' salvation.

Our maps of the world have handed us a variety of perspectives. We can hold a whole host of perspectives about different subjects, all at once. We wake up in perspectives and we go to bed in perspectives. Every waking hour of the day, we are holding a perspective about something or someone. We see the world around us, not as it truly is, but only as the way we interpret it. Our perspectives are so incredibly powerful, because our perspectives create our world and also ourselves. So much of what we believe to be "true" is only our perspective. It may be a perspective we have held for many years, but just because it's been around for a long time doesn't make it any truer, it is still just a perspective. Perhaps surprisingly at first, some of the coaching I do with my clients doesn't involve them making any real external changes at all. It doesn't involve them setting a specific goal and chasing after it or achieving any such external target. It only encompasses them making shifts to their perspectives around whatever subject it might be, because when a perspective changes, everything changes with it. When people begin to see the world and themselves in a whole new light, it means their world has truly grown already, without any circumstances moving.

Make Mountains out of Molehills

When I was a kid my mum used to talk about mountains a lot, because she used a reoccurring phrase, particularly when she thought I was being over dramatic. She would say, "You're making a mountain out of a mole hill" which is a metaphorical way of saying, "stop making a big deal out of something that is quite small and trivial". Whoever first came up with this phrase deserves a medal. To make something as gigantic as a mountain out of something as tiny as a molehill, is such a strong visual metaphor. I'm not suggesting for a minute we should be taking trivial circumstances and making them into catastrophic situations at all. I simply believe it is part of our human nature, that we can't help but make mountains out of mole hills. Our minds are wired up to make bigger the thing upon which we focus the most. In the Andes, Canessa was focussing on the difficulties, so all he saw were big, huge mountains that would get in the way. Nando was focussing on the way out, so he saw the snow-free mountains and a glorious sunset that pointed the way. Our minds do this to us all the time, even without us really knowing. They exaggerate the thing upon which we focus our attention. All of us whether we like it or not are constantly making mountains out of mole hills. Our minds eye is like the zoom focus of a camera lens and whatever we choose to focus on, our minds eye will make even bigger. When we focus on the pimple on our face, in our mind it becomes bigger; when we buy a certain type of car, suddenly we see that model on every street; when we focus on how critical our boss is, he becomes even more critical; when we focus on how fat we are, we become fatter. Whatever we focus on becomes bigger, exaggerated and more alive in our minds. There appears to be nothing we can do to stop this process; it is something our minds are wired up for. It's a natural, subconscious process for us. Our minds eye seems to have no bias with this, it doesn't care whether our perspective is focused on something helpful or unhelpful, it will still go through the same process. It has no filter only to exaggerate the positive and ignore the negative. It will make a mountain out of whatever molehill we are looking at.

"Making a mountain out of a molehill" has traditionally been used as a negative term. However, perhaps making a mountain out of a molehill can be a good thing; because if we can't stop ourselves from doing it, then we perhaps need

to learn to use it to our advantage. Maybe the key is to learn to focus our perspectives on the right molehills.

Coaching Perspectives

Working with clients, the power of perspective coaching is immense. It can change people's lives. We can hold a variety of different perspectives around the same subject. We can look at something from a variety of angles. However, I often notice that one of our perspectives tends to dominate the others, often to the point we are not even aware of the alternative perspectives we hold. It becomes the mountain perspective in our life. It's as though our dominant perspective drowns out the voice of any of the others, and yet if we are able just to pause and begin to think about alternative perspectives, we will often discover very quickly the variety of perspectives we could hold. Once we have done this, we can then begin to see which of these perspectives is most helpful for us and make the conscious choice to keep stepping into that perspective.

Lucille, a 30-year-old primary school teacher came for coaching because she hated her job and knew she needed to get out, to find a different career path for herself. She really did hate it, she was passionate in her distain for the system she had found herself working in and how, for her it had become an impossible job. However, she felt utterly stuck because what else was she qualified in, what other career was she trained for? Teaching was all she had ever known and yet she found herself in this moment of her life hating everything about it. Dragging herself into work each day was becoming increasingly difficult and her 'truth' was that she could no longer continue on this trajectory. If I was to rush with Lucille into her progress, I imagine we would have had a conversation about how she achieves the goal of changing jobs and finding her way forward in a new career. However, I'm not that kind of coach. I don't coach circumstances, I coach whole people. I was curious about Lucille's hatred and also her passion, what teaching meant for her and why she had become a teacher in the first place. I was hearing very loudly her perspective that teaching was an impossible job, but I also wanted to know what other perspectives lived within her, how else she saw teaching, herself, education and life in general. We spent a lot of time talking about Lucille's perspectives and very little, if any at all, about her progress; about how she finds a new career for herself. However, in the end Lucille did find a job she loved and a career she wanted to pursue. It was the exact same teaching job at the same school with the same class. Through our conversations Lucille completely rediscovered her love for teaching. In truth, it had never truly left her. It was just being covered over by a stronger more dominant perspective. She found within her, different ways to look at her circumstances and those different perspectives completely changed her life. On the outside, nothing really changed. Nobody would have noticed huge developments in Lucille's life, because she was professional and able to still deliver results on the outside when she was struggling on the inside. Also, I could never post on our website as an exciting testimonial, *"Coaching empowered a teacher to stay exactly where they were."* However, Lucille and I both know that our conversations and her shift in perspective completely changed her life and not only in that moment, because she now knows for ever the power of perspective and how to help herself again in the future.

Purpose Coaching

People have an inbuilt desire for purpose. We want to work at something, create something, build something, improve something but above all else know that what we are doing is purposeful. Yet so many people are living lives without truly considering the purpose behind their actions and direction.

Honey Bee Purpose

Honey Bees are incredibly purposeful. In every honey bee hive different bees have different jobs to fulfil. Nurse Bees care for the young, Guard Bees keep watch at the door to protect the hive from intruders, Construction Workers build the beeswax, Undertakers remove the dead bees from the hive, Forager Bees go out looking for pollen and nectar to feed the hive and the Queen Bee ensures the future survival of the hive by laying the eggs of the next generation. However, all these roles are fulfilled by the female bees, because male honey bees serve only one purpose. This is simply to provide the queen with sperm for fertilisation of her eggs. Honey bees seem very clear and certain of their purpose. They know exactly what they are meant to be doing and they set about making it happen. Yet, so many of us are unable to have the same clarity of purpose about the decisions and direction of our lives. As humans we are often blissfully unaware of why we do what we do.

In *Viktor Frankl's* book *Man's Search for Meaning*, he describes his experiences of the Nazi concentration camps and how people having 'meaning' to their lives was the difference between life and death. It was so powerful that as soon as people lost the meaning or purpose for staying alive, they would quite literally roll over and die. Purpose is so innately human that we must empower people to understand their own purposes in life and why they do what they do, want what they want and act how they act. Purpose at first can sound like a very grand idea and our thoughts can be drawn to the famous names of history, Nelson Mandela, Neil Armstrong or Mother Teresa, fulfilling their life purpose. Yet purpose or meaning is all around us as humans, in virtually every decision and action we take. There is purpose in the morning shower we take, the food we eat, the job we go to, the relationships we develop. We are immersed in purpose and yet we very rarely pause to consider it. *Purpose coaching* isn't necessarily about needing to make a change but rather about discovering the real purposes behind our behaviours and desires. The purpose or reason behind our actions, behaviours, hopes and decisions chart the course of our life and hold the power to enable us to either grow in a direction that benefits us, or utterly derail our lives. Unless we understand our purposes, the real 'why' behind our wants and desires, then we are at risk of moving forward in a direction that isn't really what we want or need.

The Beat of a Different Drum

Joe was an 18-year-old, handsome, straight "A", sixth form student. He was charming, athletic and unsurprisingly Head Boy of his school. Joe was referred for coaching by the Head of 6th Form because he had been displaying increasing signs of stress in the run up to the deadline for university applications. In our early conversations Joe presented as an ambitious young man, yet someone who was feeling the strain of having to make some of life's big decisions. He told me he wanted to study a law degree and work as a solicitor in a well-known firm. As Joe spoke about this, I felt my curiosity begin to rise. Something wasn't quite fitting right. The words Joe used and his tone of voice were not matching up. He was talking about his “ideal” future and yet there was very little, if any, excitement in his voice. Everything he said seemed to be coming from his left brain; it was logical and detailed and yet uninspiring. When I asked Joe how he felt about this future he had painted, his response was to tell me he didn’t find it exciting at all, but it was what he *had* to do. He went on to explain that if he wanted *“to get somewhere in life and be someone, then I have to get a proper degree and have a proper career”.*

Our following conversation went something like this…

Me – “Who is it who says you have to get a proper degree?”
Joe – “It’s just what you’re meant to do; it’s the best thing for you.”
Me – “Who says you’re meant to?”
Joe – “Just people.”
Me – “Who are these people?”

At this point Joe physically recoiled and seemed to deeply reflect upon this question. Joe knew he really wanted to work in the field of sport and exercise, but he was certain his Dad would be disappointed if he chose the degree he really wanted. Therefore, he was resigned to studying a degree and beginning a career he wasn’t very interested in but thought would win the approval of his father. Joe was, at this moment, very clearly moving forward in a way that was driven by somebody else's purpose and not his own. I have worked with so many people who are moving to the beat of someone else's drum. They are living to the purpose of someone or something else. This might not be a person, it might be a culture, an inner expectation, a societal norm, peer pressure and a whole host of other purposes that are not actually theirs.

It is vital for real growth to occur; that people have an opportunity to explore and take hold of their own purposes and clear away the imposter purposes they have adopted. We can so easily assume the purposes of others, that it can at first be tricky to separate one from the other.

In our western culture we are bombarded and saturated with messages telling us what success should look like. We should be getting richer, getting slimmer, getting promoted, going on that holiday, getting that relationship, creating that family, having those friends and buying those new clothes. Over the course of our lives these messages can quieten our own true purposes and muddy the waters for our understanding of why we are doing what we are doing and why we are moving in the direction we are.

'Should' is the most dangerous word in the English language. It carries with it a sense of oppression and demand. It is often a sure sign that what follows is something

not of our own making, but rather a purpose we have adopted somewhere else in our life. I find it useful to notice *'shoulds'* and offer them back to my clients, encouraging them to be curious about whether this is their true purpose or an imposter.

Joe went home from our coaching session that night and had a frank and honest conversation with his father. What he discovered was unexpected. It turned out his dad also wanted him to study a sports degree and he thought it was Joe, himself, who wanted to study law. Neither of them had any inclination where this idea of a law degree had come from, but both had also been assuming that this was the other's desire. I often think about how Joe's life would have moved in a very different direction, if he had been driven straight toward progress coaching without the opportunity to explore his purposes.

Purpose and Motivation

Our real purposes are immersed in motivation and if motivation is lacking, it is most likely because purpose is also lacking.

Rick was an incredible athlete in his younger years. He'd competed in endurance events, scaled mountains and paddled down enormous rivers. Now in his mid-forties he'd come for coaching because he wanted to get fit again and lose the excess weight he'd collected over the years. He tried and failed over the previous year to make any significant progress in this area of his life. It would have been easy for us to talk about the changes he wanted to make, easier still for me to assume I understood Rick's purpose for getting fit, because it would surely be about health and aging. Sure enough, when I initially asked Rick about his reasons for getting fit he confirmed it *was* about his health, but this felt a little like a 'should'. Health certainly didn't feel motivating for Rick. Yet, as we continued to speak, there was something else, something that even surprised Rick. Every time he talked about being fit, two things happened. The first was that it stirred stronger emotions within him than he anticipated and second, he kept referring in one way or another to his son. The more we talked about being fit, the more he started to speak about his son. At first Rick couldn't make sense of why he was referencing his son, because he was certain he had come to figure out how to get fit, not talk about family. After more talking, reflecting and exploring it dawned on Rick that the real purpose for him getting fit might not be about his health at all, it was more accurately that he missed spending time with his now adult son. His son was outdoorsy, adventurous and spent most of his free time in athletic pursuits and Rick desperately wanted to be with his son more. He wanted the option to be with him, whenever he could and not feel unable to spend time with him, because of his lack of fitness. The real purpose was a connection with his son and once Rick understood this his motivation levels to get fit were so much higher. This understanding of the true purpose behind his desire, changed everything for Rick, it stirred motivation in him that he hadn't known before.

For real growth to happen, people must have the space and time to explore and discover their purpose behind the growth. To create long term growth, we need motivation and that only truly comes through our purpose. Purpose Coaching is simply about being curious about the real drive behind our client's actions and goals, enabling them to explore why they are choosing the path they are on, or want to be on. It is never about giving them a sense of purpose, but rather about helping them to create awareness of the purpose that is already there. Once they are aware of their purpose, they may find the way forward changes for them, or it may simply increase their motivation down the path they are already on.

Progress Coaching

Real growth can't happen if we don't consciously do anything to create it. If purpose is about the 'why we do it' and perspective is about the 'what we see', then *progress coaching* is about the 'how we do it'. It's the bit where the action comes in. The part where people begin to explore how they are going to move forward and where all the talking converts into something to do. Progress coaching plays a vital role in the overall outcomes of a coaching relationship, but it must be kept in its place. There is no rush to get to the progress and certainly if we go there too soon, we are in danger of coaching down paths that people don't want to go. *Progress coaching* needs to take its rightful place behind perspective and purpose, so that when it kicks in it empowers people to move in directions they understand and truly want.

Coaching Progress

The question to ask ourselves all the time is *'who most wants this progress?'* The reason for this, is because it's easy to fall into the trap of wanting progress for our client, more than they want it themselves. I have seen coaches so desperate for their clients to make tangible progress; they adopt a pushing form of coaching that almost shoves clients towards progress. We must be conscious any progress has to come from the client; it must be driven and desired by them, not us. Otherwise we can end up coaching people to places they don't want to go, or certainly don't want to go so quickly.

If all coaches have to offer is *progress coaching,* the danger of pushing clients becomes even more prevalent. If progress is all we have as coaches, what happens if our clients don't make external progress? In essence, our work would become worthless. However, when we coach the whole person with their perspectives, purpose and progress, then what they take from coaching and the growth they experience happens on differing levels, it doesn't all hinge on the external progress made.

I have learnt over the years never to worry about the progress my clients are making. I used to when I first starting coaching. I had all these questions running around my head; *Is this helping them? Are they growing? Am I value for money? Will they notice the difference?* On a basic level I was worrying whether my clients were making enough progress. I once asked a client what difference coaching was making, because I wasn't sure I could see a difference. What I really meant was, I couldn't see the evidence of external progress and it was playing into my self-doubt that I wasn't doing well enough as her coach. When I asked the question, my client responded with tears and anger. "Are you joking?" she replied. "Are you seriously telling me you can't see the difference?" Then she taught me the greatest lesson I ever learnt from a client, when she spoke these words, "Just because you can't see it on the outside, it doesn't mean I haven't grown. Coaching has changed everything about me, I am utterly different on the inside. I'm set free."

These days, I don't think about progress too much, because I know it occurs naturally as part of the process. If people are given the opportunity to explore both their perspectives and purpose, then progress happens, it can't not. With human being's innate desire to grow and move forward, the progress will come when they are ready. It isn't something that has to be forced or pushed; it will flow naturally from the conversation. The irony in coaching is that the less I try and push my clients towards progress, the more they truly make. The more I create a space for them to explore and discover without the pressure of progress, the more progress they experience in a way that is exactly right for them.

Chapter 9

Two Skills – Listening & Questioning

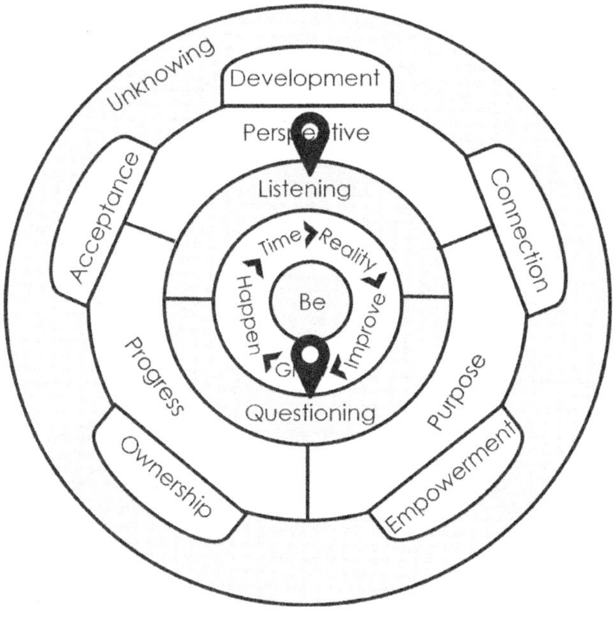

"It is our choices that show what we truly are, far more than our abilities."

J.K. Rowling, Harry Potter and the Chamber of Secrets

Trust It, You'll Know

I'm drawn to people who have bounced back in life. People who have responded to set backs and adversity with courage and honour. Bethany Hamilton is one of those people. Bethany is a world class surfer raised in Hawaii by two surf-mad parents. At just 13 years old whilst out floating on her surf board in the shallow waters of the Pacific Ocean, her left arm was bitten clean off by a shark. In the moments that followed, she lost 60% of the blood in her body and her life was only saved by the quick response of her friend's Father. Since that day, amongst other things, she returned very quickly to the water and her great love of surfing, competing again at the highest level. She became a best-selling author, inspired thousands of people from all over the world with her story and had a movie made about her life. There is a wonderful scene in *Soul Surfer,* the movie of Bethany's life, where in a moment following her recovery she seeks the wisdom of her Father about how she might manage to surf again with only one arm.

Her Father tells her, *"The greatest surfers, they all have this sixth sense, they know when the best waves are coming, they can feel it. It's a gift."*

He continues, "You know that moment between the sets, when it's quiet and the waves haven't even formed yet, it's just energy surging through the water. That's the time to be patient. Listen to your instinct, trust it, you'll know."

I feel as though he's telling her surfing is far more than just a skill, so don't worry about the fact you've lost your left arm, because real surfing doesn't just rely on your physical skills, it takes intuition, insight, instinct and trust. I've had so many similar conversations with trainee coaches wanting to know the skills of coaching and feeling as though there is something missing for them in their skill repertoire. They ask about learning new skills or techniques, as though I can teach them something in a quick ten minutes or so. I feel as though I want to respond with a plagiarism of the Soul Surfer script, *"The greatest coaches, they all have this sixth sense, they know when the best moments are coming, they can feel it. It's a gift."* and *"You know that moment between the dialogue, when its quiet and the thoughts haven't even formed yet, it's just energy surging through the connection. That's the time to be patient. Listen to your instinct, trust it, you'll know."*

Over a decade of coaching has led me to believe that there are only two skills to coaching and even then, I'm not certain they are solely skills. I still wonder if they blur the boundaries between skill and being, ability and character. Coaches must do simple practical things in the background to make coaching effective, like organisation, time management and professionalism, but the two *skills* we offer our clients are our ability to truly listen and ask helpful questions. On face value these *skills* sound easy enough to learn but they are abilities I have not yet fully mastered and don't suppose ever will.

Listening

"You is *deaf as a dumpling* compared with me!' cried the BFG. "You is hearing only thumping loud noises with those little earwigs of yours. But I am hearing all the *secret whisperings of the world*!" How right Roald Dahl was when he wrote these words because most of us, most of the time are only hearing the thumping loud noises going on in our world and yet as a coach our job is to be able to hear all the secret whisperings as well.

Listening is *the* skill of coaching. It is also the skill of being human. There is nothing more important for a coach or human to do, than to truly listen to people. Yet listening is a hugely underrated skill in our day to day lives. Perhaps we don't pause long enough to fully grasp the power it holds. Listening makes people feel something, it stirs emotions within them; it has the power to make them feel as though they are the most important person in the world, yet also the power to make them feel utterly worthless. There is no middle ground with listening. When a person feels deeply listened to and completely understood, it is as though they matter, they are understandable. Steven Covey put it beautifully when he wrote *"Few needs of the human heart are greater than the need to be understood - to have a voice that is heard, respected and valued."* Yet when a person is not listened to or understood, when they feel unheard, it destroys something inside of them, it robs them of something of themselves. Nick Luxmore, who spent his career as a teacher and then many more years as a school's counsellor, argues that being understood is what actually creates and moulds our self-esteem. He states, *"The process of listening and trying to understand young people is so important because it offers the attunement which some young people haven't experienced earlier in their lives....a positive sense of one's self (self-esteem) comes from being understandable and being understood."* Therefore, when we are truly listening to people we are not only understanding their words, but more importantly enhancing their self-worth. When we are not listening, it is not so much the misunderstanding that is the real issue, but more the eroding of a person's sense of their own value that can make poor listening so destructive.

Listening has a huge impact on the way our clients feel when they are with us and therefore on the effectiveness of the coaching. Henry Kimsey-House and his colleagues describe the effect of listening in this way, *"People open up when they know they're really being listened to; they expand; they have more presence. They feel safer and more secure as well and trust grows."* For us, as coaches, to be effective in our work then the ability to listen deeply is paramount. I find that as I listen to my clients, something starts to develop within them and the process of growth begins, often with very little, if any, intervention from myself. My first aim as a coach, is to understand my client's world through their eyes and to fully do that, I must find the discipline to not look at their world through my own eyes.

The Levels of listening

There are many levels at which we can listen, but I have grouped these into just four deepening layers, *distracted, filtered, attentive* and *attuned.*

Distracted Listening

Perhaps much of what we describe as listening in our busy daily lives, is in fact no more than distracted listening. A half listening, where we are paying some attention to what the speaker is saying, but we also have our thoughts on something else. This kind of listening is clear to see when we are holding a conversation whilst engaged in another activity such as watching the TV, reading a book or sending an email. Our concentration is on a task whilst also partially on the speaker's words. This kind of distracted listening is obvious to us, because despite our attempts to look as though we are listening by throwing in some fleeting eye contact and the occasional “umhum”, it is clear half our attention is elsewhere. However, distracted listening also occurs when we are simply consumed with other thoughts in our mind. We’re not physically engaged in another activity, but rather mentally elsewhere, thinking about other issues rather than what the speaker is saying. This kind of distracted listening is harder to spot, as we are likely to be physically doing all the right things, like maintaining eye contact, nodding at the correct moment and even asking the occasional question. Yet, we are not truly listening. For me, this kind of distracted listening was a skill that I mastered throughout school. I could sit in class, bored by the teacher and the subject, yet doing everything to look like I was listening. My mind would be thinking about the good-looking girl on the front row, the football match I played at break-time or what I might be having for my dinner, whilst throughout I was able to maintain the posture of a young man who looked like he was paying attention. I spent class after class, week after week and year after year mastering the art of distracted listening. Although we might believe as a distracted listener we are doing a good job of looking like we are listening, the reality is that our speakers know we are not truly with them. It’s important to recognise that whoever is speaking to us is a master of reading body language. They have been subconsciously interpreting body language from the moment they were born, so we must accept they will know when we are distracted and not truly listening. It might just be a flicker of the eyes, a stifled yawn or a glazed over look. When we are distracted in our listening, despite our best efforts, we can't really hide it. Our body will somehow give the game away and our speaker will know we are not fully listening to them. At school, my teachers knew, because from time to time they would call me out of my distracted listening by directing a question straight at me, "What do you think about that? JOHN!" And wow, did it make me jump as I scrambled around my mind for the words my teacher had just been saying and an answer that might save the embarrassment of my distracted mind. Distracted listening is no use at all to a coach or a client, because a distracted listener can hear the words a speaker is saying but has no chance of really understanding any meaning behind those words. If our client notices, and they will, that we are distracted they will begin to shut down, say less and never speak with any depth. We cannot be an effective coach if we are not fully present with our clients, so we must learn to leave all distractions, whether physical or mental at the door of the coaching room and find a place where we can truly be with our client. John Whitmore wrote, *"Perhaps the hardest thing a coach needs to learn to do is to shut up!"* I believe coaches must exercise the discipline of not only shutting up at times, but more importantly shutting their minds from the distractions of their own world and life.

Filtered Listening

Even when we are listening to our client and we are not in a place of distraction, we very often find ourselves listening in a filtered way. This is the sense in which we are filtering everything our client says through our own map of the world. As a filtered listener, we are able to hear our client's words, but we can only give them meaning by taking those words and placing them firmly into our world. This means we are only able to understand what our client's words might mean for us, and in doing so, we are at risk of completely misinterpreting what those words mean for them. Filtered listening is so often the cause of communication breakdown in our day to day lives. How many times do we hear, "Oh I thought you meant", "you've taken it the wrong way" or "that wasn't my intention," even during a conversation where two people are attempting to listen to each other? Words carry so much variation in meaning, that if we don't try and understand what a word, sentence or story means for our clients, then we are never truly able to listen to them. The meaning of words change through generations, cultures and regions. I remember a few years ago taking some teenagers to see a pantomime where one of the characters was introduced to the audience as the "Wicked Queen". As she entered the stage, boos and hisses rang out amongst the crowd, when one of the teenagers in our party lent over to me and asked, "why are they booing the Wicked Queen?"

Slightly bemused by the question I replied, "because she's wicked". Then it dawned on me that in teenage culture at this time, if something was "good" it was "wicked"; if they liked something they didn't refer to it as brilliant or fantastic, they called it "wicked". It made no sense at all in this young person's world that a "Wicked Queen" would be booed and he had no knowledge at all, of the original meaning of the word wicked. Imagine a coaching session where our client uses the word wicked and we as the coach filter it through our world and believe we know what they mean. Now imagine a coaching session where our client talks about family or confidence or success and we assume we know what those words mean, because we filter them through our own map. What confusion and misunderstanding might follow.

We will notice filtered listening in ourselves, when our clients speak of something in their world, yet we create a picture of our own world. When perhaps a client talks about their family and we imagine our family, when they speak of their boss and we see our old boss or when they talk of being in love and we remember our own feelings of being in love.

Filtered listeners are constantly checking their own map of the world, in order to make sense of the speaker's world. Yet effective listening happens as a coach when we are able to put our own map away and listen solely and completely to our client's map. As coaches we must listen without our own maps involved. We must attempt to understand our client's words through the meaning they are intending, not the interpretation we are placing upon them. If we listen in a filtered way, we can never truly understand the meaning behind our client's words and we can never really invite them into a place of trust where they are fully *"being understandable and being understood."*

Attentive Listening

Attentive listening is when our attention is fully on our client and their map of the world. As a coach we are in a place where our map is put aside, our complete focus is with our client and we are embracing every word they say. Attentive listening often occurs for us when we are listening to a riveting speaker, watching an important part of a movie or when someone is telling us something we know we really need to remember. I notice myself in my day-to-day life suddenly become a very attentive listener when I am about to embark on a new activity that carries some risk, like white water rafting or abseiling. At that moment, when the instructor is telling me the do's and don'ts of the safety procedures, I become an extremely attentive listener, mainly because I want to know how not to die.

Attentive listening can be very useful for coaches, particularly at moments when we are feeling tired, have other distractions going on in life or for some reason find a client difficult to listen to. It enables us to get into a listening zone with our clients where we are fully focused on them and their words. However, attentive listening is also somewhat like a version of "tunnel-vision listening", as though we are listening with blinkers on. We are so attentive to what our speaker is verbally saying and visually doing, that our listening becomes blinkered in a way that means we may be missing so much of what they are really trying to communicate. Our clients not only communicate to us through their words, tone of voice and body language but also through what they are not saying, because what they are not saying (the thing they are maybe consciously or even unconsciously avoiding) might well be the most important aspect they need to communicate. If we offer our clients attentive listening, we will be giving them an experience far greater than they may experience in their everyday lives and yet there is still a greater depth to which, we as coaches, can go in our listening.

Attuned Listening

Attuned listening is the ability to completely tune into the other person. It is deeper, wider and more holistic than attentive listening and creates a level of understanding that surpasses words, tone and even body language. An attuned listener hears not only the words, but the spaces between the words, not only the tone of voice but the tone of true meaning, not only the facial expressions, but what those expressions might be masking and not only the setting, but what is happening outside of the setting. In Erin Meyer's insightful book, The Culture Map, she recalls how one of her Japanese clients describes their ability to listen, *"In Japan, we implicitly learn, as we are growing up, to communicate between the lines and to listen between the lines when others are speaking…if you can't read the air, you are not a good listener."* In order to begin to listen at this depth, in a way that we can 'read the air' of our clients, there are a number of aspects that can be helpful to understand.

Attuned listening is curious

In order to be an attuned listener with our clients we must possess oodles of curiosity. Henry Kimsey-House and his colleagues describe curiosity as "open, inviting, spacious, almost playful." Curiosity is not at all nosey, a curious coach isn't interested in knowing the facts of a situation, or the "who did what" of our client's circumstances. To be curious is to hold a desire to go exploring with our clients, to always be open to new possibilities and greater awareness. Curious coaches aren't cynical or sceptical, they are trusting of their client, yet they are always wondering what else might be going on? To be curious is to truly enter our client's map of the world and wonder what else is there that is yet to be seen, discovered or understood. Yet to be curious also means to have the ability to empty ourselves of our own presumptions and interpretations of what our clients' words and world might mean. Curiosity and analysis don't ever live within the same coaching space. Curiosity leaves no room at all for the analysing of our clients because as soon as a coach begins analysis of a client's words, they have immediately stopped being curious and ultimately stopped listening. Analysis comes from a place of trying to know what the answer is, trying to find the "right" meaning for something and sticking a diagnosis of sorts onto our clients; whereas curiosity starts with not knowing and being okay with that sense of the unknown, yet wanting to uncover and explore again and again.

Attuned listening doesn't know

What so often gets in the way of our listening with our clients is our filtered listening and our assumption that we know what they mean. This assumption often comes from a place of us instantly connecting our clients' words to something we have heard before. Almost an *"Oh I know what this is because I have heard this before"* attitude that creates so much misunderstanding and misinterpretation of what our client really means and is truly trying to communicate.

Attuned listening starts and remains in a place of not knowing.

The most helpful sense of not-knowing is found within the theory of Phenomenology, which was first developed by Edmund Husserl early in the 20th Century and then progressed by a variety of followers. In a very simplified sense, Phenomenology is concerned with the way in which we experience and interpret the world around us. There are some helpful rules within the Phenomenological Method for us as coaches, that can enable us to remain truly listening to our clients' experience. Ernesto Spinelli presents us a simplified description of one of the most helpful rules, the Rule of Epoche which *"urges us to impose an 'openness' on our immediate experience... so that our subsequent interpretations of it may prove to be more adequate."* The Rule of Epoche is also referred to as 'Bracketing'. It is the ability to '*bracket'* our previous interpretations, in a sense to be able to listen to our clients as though we are hearing something for the very first time. It's as though we have placed brackets around this transaction with our client and we keep out any previous experience or interpretation of what our client is saying.

A few years ago, during the Autumn I, along with a group of other parents, took our children along to the public park in the middle of our town, where amongst the play area, fountain and open greenery there were several horse-chestnut trees. As we arrived at the entrance to the park, one of the older children asked if they could go looking for the fallen fruits of the horse chestnut tree, more commonly known as conkers. All the other children, a group of about ten ranging in age from 4 to 9 years old, quickly became excited at the thought of finding these big, rotund conkers strewn all over the grassy banks and tarmac paths. As a group, we agreed and quickly made our way over to the biggest of all the conker trees at the far end of the park. When the kids enthusiastically began a chant of *"let's find conkers, let's find conkers"* as we cantered our way across the grass, my four-year-old son had a very important question for me. We had adopted him almost a year earlier and as my two older children ran ahead with the bigger kids, my boy tugged at my hand to get my attention and simply asked, *"Daddy, what is a conker?"* I hadn't realised he had no idea at all of what a conker might be. He was excited at the prospect of finding one but didn't even know what he might be looking for. I had held conkers in my hand every Autumn since before I could remember and my two older children had done the same, so I assumed my little boy, at the age of four, would know exactly what a conker was. Yet, he had no idea, nothing, not even an assumption or guess. All he knew was that other children seemed to find conkers exciting. He was in such a beautifully curious, not-knowing place where all other experience or assumption of what a conker might be, was not present within his world. He didn't even need to "bracket" anything in that moment as he had nothing contaminating his understanding of a conker. He was completely open to the possibility of a conker being anything and this is precisely how I strive to be when I listen to my clients

One of the best listeners I ever had the pleasure to work with was Shelia Smith, a Counsellor and Supervisor based in Sheffield. I observed Shelia listening to individuals and groups of people in a way that intrigued me. She seemed to be able to attune herself with people in a way that was purer and richer than I had witnessed before. When I asked her what her secret to this remarkable ability to listen was, she simply answered, *"I start from the place of holding nothing."* I love this idea of listening in way in which we hold nothing. Even though our clients may be speaking words we have heard before, I want to receive those words as though I have nothing, no assumption, no prejudice, no analysis, just curiosity about possibilities, what they are really trying to communicate and what that means for them. I'm not suggesting this is completely possible as Spinelli reminds us that, *"phenomenologists themselves have pointed out repeatedly no final or complete act of bracketing can ever be achieved, nor should we trust any claim to have done so."* However, I do believe that this must be an aspirational goal for all effective coaches to always reach for.

Attuned listening also leaves no room for disappointment or frustration. We can only be disappointed if we have a previous expectation with which our experience doesn't match. By being curious, we have no expectations by which to be disappointed. If my son had assumed that a conker was some kind of amazing sweet shop, or a super-fast bike or a Disney theme park, he would most probably have been disappointed or frustrated by what is effectively a hard, brown nut. Yet when he found his first conker, he was delighted by what he held in his hand and curious again about all the possible things he might be able to use it for. Attuned listening is never disappointed with what it finds, it is only ever curious again and again and can never be disappointed or let down.

Attuned listening also listens to self

Attuned listening is about understanding what is happening for the client, but also about what is happening for yourself. Attuned listeners hear, sense and feel their client whilst also hearing, sensing and feeling themselves; not in a way which distracts from the client but actually adds value to their experience of really being listened to. As a coach it is not about being distracted by our own map or filtering the client's words through our map. Rather it is about being attuned to what is going on for us, within this moment, with this client. Often much of what is being communicated, is being done subconsciously. As a coach we may only ever pick that up through what we sense inside ourselves and what our intuition is telling us. We must therefore be able to notice and listen to what is going on for us as the coach, as well as what is going on for our client.

Working with one client I became aware I had the sensation of him drawing close to me as he shared something of his life and then he would pull away, almost immediately withdrawing from me. This didn't happen in a physical sense, but rather at an emotional level. I didn't really know exactly what I was feeling, but I decided to offer it to my client. Not in an analytical way, just simply sharing what I was sensing and whether it might be helpful for him. I hadn't heard him do this, I had felt him do this and I believe my feelings are just as capable at listening as my ears. My client's response was to breathe a huge sigh of relief and tell me this is a pattern he repeats in almost every relationship he holds, and it is something he really wants to move forward with. Because I had felt him communicating this with me and shared it with him our coaching relationship became a much richer soil for development and growth.

As an attuned listener, we must be attuned to ourselves and what is being transmitted by our client on the silent frequency that we can only pick up amongst our own feelings and intuition. It is a process of learning to trust ourselves and only ever offering to our client what we hear in a speculative way and never as an analysis of what is going on.

To be a truly attuned listener takes a deep desire and want to be immersed in somebody else's interpretation of their world and a discipline to leave our own interpretations well alone. Steven Covey summed it up beautifully when he wrote, *"you listen with your ears, but you also and more importantly, listen with your eyes and with your heart. You listen for feeling, for meaning. You listen for behaviour. You use your right brain as well as your left. You sense, you intuit, you feel."*

Questioning

Left to our own devices, we humans are curious beings. We can't help ourselves! We've looked across seas and wondered what might be over there, we've studied the heavens, craving answers to the *whys* and *whats* of the universe, we've delved into our past and dreamed up our futures and in all of this we are asking question after question.

Questions are everywhere in human existence and relationship. In virtually every conversation and interaction, questions are lurking and we've been immersed in them since the beginning of our lives. However, my early relationship with questions was greatly affected by my school experience. I began my existence so very curious about the world, wondering and pondering, doubting and knowing, asking questions that mattered and questions that didn't, yet all the time encouraged by the adults around me to be inquisitive. As I moved up beyond the early years of education, this encouragement to ask curious questions seemed to be replaced by the implicit understanding to only ask 'sensible' questions or 'good' questions. It seemed I began to learn the imposed 'rules' of questioning, where some questions were wrong or simply not what I was expected to ask. If I had let it, my inquisitiveness would have slowly been replaced with an ability to only ever ask information gathering questions. Questions that helped me know facts, that created a transfer of knowledge from the teacher to myself, that enabled me to get the 'right' answer. I was in danger of slowly but surely being drained of my natural curious questioning and replacing it with an ability to solely gather facts and deduce answers. Henry Kimsey-House and colleagues tell us this experience in school of asking questions to *"enable us to deduce answers"* meant that *"we learned that questions are used to narrow the possibilities."* How incredible that questions, with all their potential for exploration and discovery were presented to us as a way to narrow and not broaden possibilities. Alongside this, I was also learning British social norms that some questions were too personal, too difficult, too curious, too revealing and not the types of questions people were expecting to be faced with. It felt as though there were very socially acceptable questions, such as "how has your day been?", "how's the family?" or "how is work going?", but certainly not "what do you really love in life?", "how do you really feel?", or "what are you really brilliant at?"

Due to our early relationship with questions, at first glance, when faced with the question of why we ask questions, it might appear the answer is purely to gather information, to deduce answers or to gain understanding. Yet, if we can do away with our conditioning around questions and truly examine the reasons people ask questions and the purpose of questions, we discover a diverse range of motives. These include curiosity, nosiness, information gathering, learning, checking understanding, manipulation, belittling, embarrassing, displaying empathy, filling silence, politeness, rapport building, flirting, making requests and even giving commands, along with a whole host of other possibilities.

Amongst the plethora of questions we have ever been asked in our lives, I am curious how many have really stood out for us? How many have had great impact on our lives? How many have been a catalyst for growth? During my early adult life, in the shadows of my childhood, my own answer to that question would have probably been only a handful. I think the quality of questions we experience are perhaps lacking because our educational experience and social norms have prevented us from asking questions which really matter and make a difference to people. When I came across coaching, I discovered a place where the curiosity in me could be released again, where the questions I ask could be full of wonder and inquisitiveness once more. Where there was no such thing as a 'right' or 'wrong' question and in becoming a coach, I have found myself in places where these impactful questions occur much more frequently for me. Through having coaching, going to supervision, attending training and generally hanging out with people who ask me the types of questions which make me think, allow me to explore and shift my perspective, the quality of questions in my life has grown astronomically. I love a truly great question that creates movement in me, a question I have never been asked before that takes me to new depths of awareness and growth. Questions hold the potential to grow people, to be the catalyst of transformation, the opener of eyes and the gateway to new possibilities. Great questions remind me of the wardrobe door CS Lewis takes Lucy through on her journey to Narnia, where she discovers a whole new land of hope, fear, power and vulnerability waiting for her on the other side. Without the wardrobe door Lucy remains in the old house, safe and secure, yet blind to her own potential, adventure and strength. Yet questions can also be the container for social niceties, the prison cell that holds us in the same place we have always been, the buoyancy aid that keeps us only on the surface of our life, unable to plunge to the depths of awareness and understanding which would allow us to access more of our true greatness.

Head and Heart Questions

There are many names for the type of questions which carry impact and cut beneath the surface. Nancy Kline speaks about '*Incisive Questions*' which *"remove limiting assumptions, freeing the mind to think afresh". The* Co-Active Coaching Model describes '*Powerful Questions*' which *"invite introspection, present additional solutions and lead to greater creativity and insight."* Over the years I have come to simply refer to quality questions as '*Heart Questions*'. The reason for this is two-fold; firstly, because I see people find their responses to these questions not in the logical, factual part of their brain, but rather in their hearts. Secondly, these questions are directed not at the details of the client's story, but rather towards the heart of the matter. In contrast, '*Head Questions*' are the information questions, the fact gathering questions which clients can answer instantly, because they can access the information almost immediately in the memory part of their brain. '*Head Questions*' make no real difference to a person, they don't change anything or take them anywhere. There is no exploration or creative thought with '*Head Questions*', there is simply the transfer of information from the client to the coach.

For example, Head Questions around the subject of parenting might look like this…

Do you have children?
How many?
What ages are they?

In answering these, nothing will change for a client; there will be no movement of thought, no shift in perspective and no discovery of any kind. They will simply be able to reply with facts.

Heart Questions around the subject of parenting might look like this…

What are your hopes and dreams for your children?
What's your greatest achievement as a parent?
When do you feel most connected to your children?

There are no definitive facts with '*Heart Questions'* and therefore no 'right' or 'wrong' answer, there is simply an open space for the client to explore and work with. These questions are unlikely to be answered in an instant, because they are not answered from the logical brain, but rather from the heart and therefore require wondering, creativity and exploration. *'Heart Questions'* also stir some degree of emotive response from our clients, they carry with them a sense of connection to the feeling part of our being. This is important because as human beings we are emotional creatures and more often than not, our motivation to action is driven far more by our emotions than our logic. *'Heart Questions'* do something which *'Head Questions'* can never do, they empower people to really feel the subject, to make sense of it emotionally, as well as logically. They enable clients to line up their heart with their head, their emotions with their logic, to create congruence in themselves, which allows them to move forward with greater awareness of why they are heading in this chosen direction.

Striking a CORD

'Heart Questions' have a number of subtle components and a simple way to remember these is to recognize that they strike a CORD, which stands for Clean, Open, Resonating and Direct.

Clean simply means that heart questions are pure. They are not leading anywhere and there is no hidden agenda. They are not looking for the client to answer in a particular way or worded to coerce the client to say what they think might be expected of them.

Open describes the principle that heart questions can't be answered with 'yes' or 'no', they require more exploration and thought from a client. They open up the conversation rather than close it down.

Resonating is the idea that heart questions have some emotional charge with them, they are not just asked to our logic, but also to our emotions. When a question is resonating with a client, we will see something, which might be tears or smiles, a clenched fist or shuffling in their seat, but we will see some kind of physical reaction.

Direct is a sense of asking *heart questions* in their simplest form. This is not the same as being directive, but rather not having to fill questions with waffle, justifications or explanation. It's the straight forward asking of a direct, to the point, question.

Fear of the Next Question

Many trainee coaches seem to fear asking questions more than listening. This is probably because our questions are 'on show' much more than our listening. I see new coaches worrying that either they will ask the 'wrong' questions, or they won't have a question to ask at all. However, if we truly learn to trust our clients to discover their own answers, we will begin to see that they virtually ask themselves the questions as well. If we can truly listen to our clients, we will start to hear the next question hidden within their words. They will headline and emphasize certain words, phrases or points, as if saying to us, “go on, ask me about that.” It’s as though these headlines light up when they are speaking. Often the question a person most needs, can be found in their own words.

Another aspect of questioning is simply reflecting a client’s own words back to them as a question which can have a profound impact. For example, if a client says, “I always mess it up” and the coach reflects back “You always mess it up?” This can create a whole new level of conversation and thought for the client. Hearing their own words back, enables them to find a fresh perspective on their beliefs, realities and development. Reflections are so simple, yet incredibly powerful for people.

I used to believe I needed to work hard at the specific wording or phrasing of a question, so I would fret that one particular word might change the whole dynamic of the question. These days, I tend not to worry about this because I believe it is sufficient in any given moment to offer the best question we have to our client and if it is not ‘perfectly’ worded, they will take the question and convert it into the exact right question for them. As long as we are listening and offering the best we have back to our clients then that, in that moment, is enough. The wording of questions will come with time and experience, but it will never be 'perfect', it can't be, it will only be enough in that moment to give our clients chance to explore and grow.

Silence

Sometimes the best you can offer to your client is not a question at all. It is silence. Silence is incredibly underrated in the process of growth. When working with people, we can be so conscious of our next question, that we jump in immediately after they have finished talking, but often what people need is just, as Margaret Crompton tells us, *"a few feet of silence".*

People often don't say all of what they were intending to say. They wrap things up early for fear of over-talking or sounding like they are waffling. A new question in this instance, can take the conversation in a different direction. If I get a hint my client has more to say, I will often let silence linger in order to give them opportunity to continue without any intervention from me. It's incredible to see the amount of times where silence is offered and my clients fill this space with more of their story, more of their reflections. Mark Prever described it in this way, *"Intervening too early deprives ...an opportunity for deeper exploration and experiencing, so often not found in normal day-to-day conversation where people take turns in speaking and where silence is rare or imbued with meaning."*

Silence plays a vital role in the process of growth, but it can be an experience that is unusual or even awkward for us. Many of us have been conditioned to fill silence and see silence as a negative or disconnect between people. Yet, for people to really explore and initiate growth in their lives, silence is one of their greatest friends. People who aren't ready or willing to grow avoid silence. Silence often comes hand in hand with thought and reflection. Many people in our world don't want to think, because if they think, they are worried about what they might discover. They keep themselves busy; they avoid silence in any form, even when they are alone. People who want to and are ready to develop, need silence and to not offer silence in the process of growth, would be like leaving the yeast out of the recipe for bread. When our clients are silent because they are reflecting, it is important to hold the silence they need, to do the thinking that needs to be done. Nancy Kline refers to this as 'The Thinking Space" which she describes like this, *"When people are quiet in this way, they are busy. They are off on a solitary 'walk'. You have not been invited to come along, but it is assumed that you will be there when they come back. They will want to tell you about where they have been. Their 'walk' is of high quality exactly because they know you are waiting, thinking about them, while they are 'gone'. This is a privileged moment for you; don't ruin it"*

Chapter 10

BRIGHT Framework – The Scaffolding and the Stabilisers

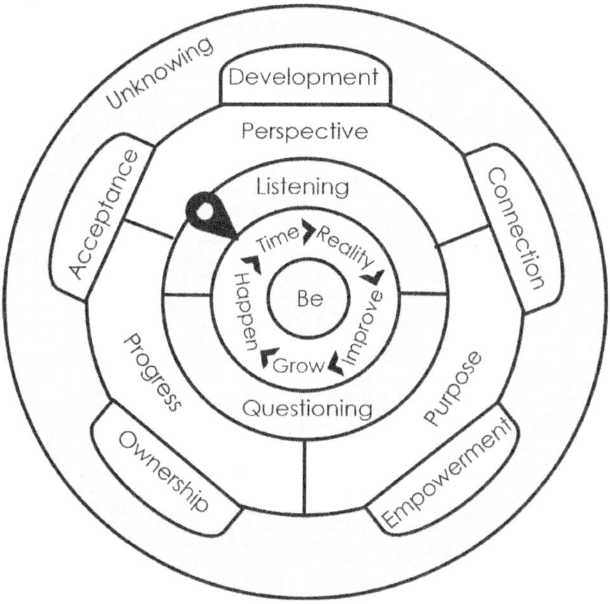

"When one puts up a building one makes an elaborate scaffold to get everything into its proper place. But when one takes the scaffold down, the building must stand by itself with no trace of the means by which it was erected."

Andres Segovia

The Liberty Scaffolding

"It's probably been the most photographed scaffolding in the world", said Harold O'Callaghan Jr, the President of Universal, the firm responsible for erecting the scaffolding around the Statue of Liberty, while it was restored to its former glory, between 1984 and 1986. At the time, it was the largest scaffolding ever built and the scaffolding company were given three principal requirements to adhere to whilst erecting the scaffolding; it had to withstand 100 mph winds, the statue had to be visible during the restoration work and the scaffolding had to be free standing, not touching the statue itself. Normally scaffolding is tied into the building it is there to support, but in this case, it had to stand free from the structure, it had to stand up by itself. However, none of these were actually the most problematic part of the job, because as Callaghan goes on to explain, "Usually the most difficult part is putting up the scaffolding, but taking it down from around the statue was tricky because of the special care we had to take not to mar the statue's skin."

There are a number of parallels that can be drawn between this story of the Statue of Liberty's scaffolding and the BRIGHT coaching framework I have developed.

It's Just Scaffolding

Although the Statue of Liberty's scaffolding became iconic itself for the years it was up and was a great feat of engineering, it was just scaffolding. I know many people, including myself, who since 1986 have been to visit the Statue of Liberty and none of us have been disappointed that the scaffolding wasn't there anymore. We didn't go to see the scaffolding; we went to see the statue. It is the statue that is the main thing, the scaffolding, as impressive as it was, was only ever there in a supporting role. A coaching model, if we're not mindful, can become a rigid process which is 'done' to people and something that, while we are following, gives us a sense of doing the 'correct' thing. I worry that we, as coaches, will put our trust in a framework, rather than in ourselves, our clients and the connection between us. Its important to always remember that any coaching framework or model is just a scaffolding and never the main event.

The Client Must Be Visible

In the same way that the Statue of Liberty had to be visible during the time the scaffolding was up, so our coaching clients must always be visible through our coaching framework. I have seen coaches so rigid in their working style that the client is lost somewhere in the midst of frameworks, models and theories. This is so backwards, because all of this stuff is simply there to serve the growth of the client. The client and their needs must always take precedent over any framework or structure the coach may have and if the client is ever playing second fiddle to a framework or model, there is something out of balance.

Taking it down can be the hardest part

Scaffolding makes me nervous, because often as soon as we are given a scaffolding or framework for anything, it can become something we grow dependent upon. When my daughter was learning to ride her bike, she had two stabilising wheels attached and rode around happily on these for months. Without her knowing, I gradually over time, raised the stabilisers off the ground, to the point where they were still attached to the bike but weren't actually serving any purpose. She was riding around without either stabiliser ever touching the ground. When the time came to take off the stabilisers, my daughter couldn't be without them. Suddenly, because these supporting wheels were no longer there, she felt like she couldn't ride anymore and was going to fall off. Even though the stabilisers had done nothing of any use for months and she was more than capable of keeping her balance without them, she felt she needed them. In the same way, I have been nervous about creating a coaching framework for people, because I worry a coaching framework can become a pair of stabilisers that coaches can't be without. Once we have a scaffolding; it can be hard for us to take down and yet it is imperative that as soon as the framework is no longer needed, we discard it immediately.

The BRIGHT Framework

Due to this, even though, over time, I had become aware of certain elements that existed within coaching conversations and in my own mind had formulated them into a framework, I resisted sharing it or teaching it to anyone else for years. I sensed danger in educating people in something that looks like a model. However, I began to realise this could be a useful teaching tool for new coaches setting out on the journey of helping people grow. Simply like the stabilisers on a bicycle, which help a child keep upright whilst they learn how to balance themselves, this framework can be helpful for new coaches to find their balance. It is not something experienced coaches will ever think about, use or need but can certainly provide some stepping stones for people in the early days. This framework has come to be known as BRIGHT and is where the type of coaching I provide got its name. It is a completely flexible framework that supports and assists the coach, rather than ever being a strict structure that must be followed. It's just scaffolding.

The BRIGHT framework is made up of the different parts that exist within a coaching conversation. It's simplistic and yet, as we'll discover, also gives us great depth within coaching. We'll explore this depth in the following chapters, but as a brief introduction this is what BRIGHT looks like on the surface.

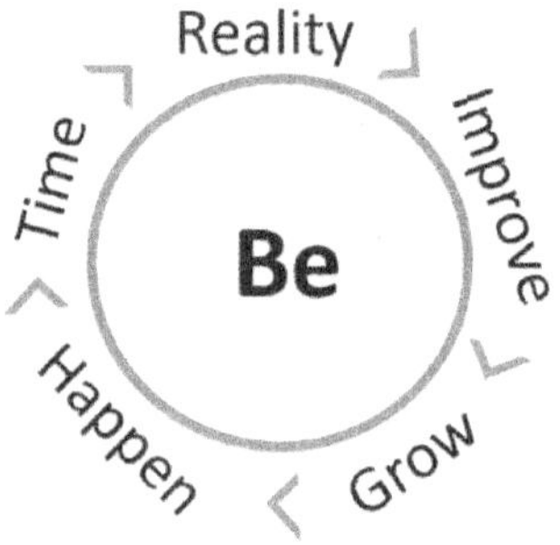

Be – Being fully present and being in the moment

This is the most important part of any coaching. Learning to simply be with our client is the heartbeat of coaching and more important than any other part of this framework, which is why it sits right at the centre of all the others.

Reality - What is our client's present reality?

The first part of coaching is often to know where the client is starting. We must get interested and curious about our client's present reality and discover what is going on for them right now. It's all about seeing and feeling the world the way our client sees and feels their reality and never about how we think they should see and feel it.

Improve - What area of life does our client want to improve?

This is the part of the framework that focusses the coaching on a specific area. It is crucial in coaching that there is a clear, distinct focus because growing takes time. It is always led by the client and never determined by the coach.

Grow - How does our client want to grow in this area?

This aspect enables the coach and client to discover what it is the client really wants. It creates vision for the client and is the part that people in everyday conversations often skip.

Happen - What is our client going to make happen to move this forward?

This is simply about what the client is going to do to make progress. It is about turning the talk into actions. Having said that, this doesn't always have to be an action, because sometimes our clients may need more time to think about something, or spend some time reflecting.

Time - What timescale is our client working to?

This is the part of the framework that ensures our clients commit to a determined timeframe with the actions they set for themselves. It also ensures our clients stay accountable for their development.

Although on paper this framework follows a process from reality, to improve, to grow, to happen, to time, there is no rule that this is exactly how a coaching conversation should play out. These are simply the elements that I believe exist within coaching, but they can and do happen in all sorts of orders and often dance around from one to another. I have never shared this framework with a client, as I don't believe it adds any benefit to them, it is purely a teaching framework for new coaches, to give them a scaffolding whilst they find their own balance with coaching.

Chapter 11

Be - Just Being

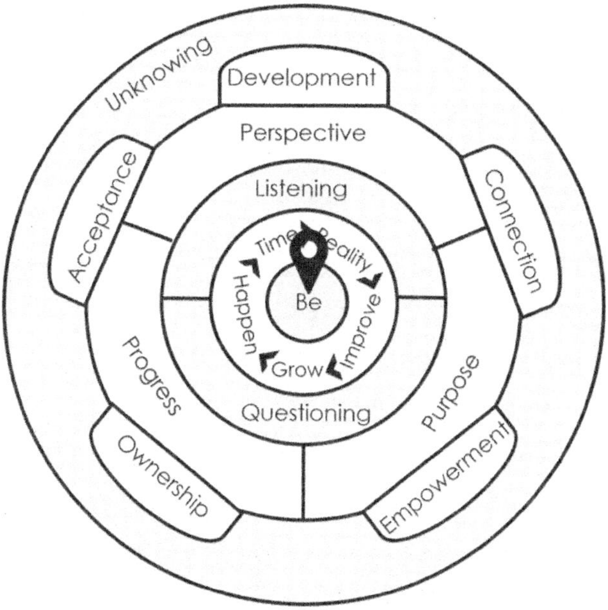

"When Morrie was with you, he was really with you. He looked you straight in the eye, and he listened as if you were the only person in the world"

"I believe in being fully present", Morrie said. "That means you should be with the person you're with."

Mitch Albom, Tuesdays with Morrie

Presence

In the long-awaited sequel to Peter Pan, the boy that never grew up had grown up. He'd become middle aged, married Wendy's granddaughter and now had children of his own. Robin Williams' wonderful portrayal in the movie *Hook,* of this adult version of Peter Pan as a driven business man, living far from Neverland, struggling to find anything resembling a work life balance, teaches us a deep truth about human relationships. In his striving over the years to make a 'better life' for his family, he had gathered wealth and status, yet lost the one thing his family wanted more than anything else. He had gone seeking riches and in doing so had lost the real treasure.

In an attempt to lure Peter Pan back to Neverland, his old adversary Captain Hook kidnaps his children and taunts Peter to once again engage in warfare with him. As Peter, on a rescue mission, arrives in his old stomping ground, he quickly finds himself taken captive by The Lost Boys. His former gang struggle to believe this wrinkled, serious, grown up before them, was ever the daring, playful Peter Pan. As the story unfolds, The Lost Boys, help this obsessive businessman go on an internal journey of his own. Reconnecting with his past and the truths he once knew, he is reminded time and again that The Lost Boys, his children, his wife, Wendy and even Tinkerbell want nothing from him, other than his presence. They simply want him to be there, with them, wherever that might be. It is a portrayal of the oldest truth of human relationships. Our presence and our ability to simply *be* with another person is the greatest treasure we can ever give and receive. We are often not too dissimilar to a grown-up Peter Pan, our wonderful ability to be, that we once possessed in abundance as a child, has been over shadowed by the doing of our lives. In all our striving after activity and possessions, we have somewhere lost the art of '*being*'.

How often in our daily life are we able to truly and fully 'be' with another human? I don't mean physically be in the presence of someone, that's easy and straight forward enough for most of us. I mean 'be' in a fully present way, a wholly in the moment way where we are completely engaged with the other person. 'Be' is the most important part of coaching and there is nothing that will ever take precedence over our capacity as a coach to 'be' with another person. Not incredible listening skills, nor beautifully worded questions, not insightful intuition, nor captivating rapport, not action-setting, not accountability, not ownership or any other 'attribute' of coaching, will ever come close to the importance of simply being with our client. It is the most precious of gifts we can ever offer another person and it is where the true depth and power of all human connections lie. It is the ability to 'be' with our clients, to 'be' fully present in the moment and to 'be' completely ourselves, that enables the coaching relationship to take effect.

It would be easy to assume that 'being' comes effortlessly to us and yet our world and upbringings have so often been consumed with 'doing', that we have lost our capacity to be. So many trainee coaches come onto our coaching courses expecting to be taught the 'doing' parts of how to coach. The skills, techniques and tools are what is at the forefront of their learning ambitions and although they certainly acquire some of these things, they are not and never should be, the main event in coach education. The skills of coaching prove virtually useless unless coaches are also able to grasp the 'being' aspect of coaching.

The ability and importance of 'being' stretches way beyond the realms of coaching. Imagine a world where leaders are truly engaged with their teams, imagine parents able to just 'be' with their children, imagine friends being fully present with one another and imagine teachers 'being' in the moment with their pupils. In every walk of life, in every human relationship, there is the burning need within us to simply have another person who can 'be' with us.

Being with someone has a purifying effect on the relationship. It clears a path for real connection. It's as though all distortion has been tuned out and there is a beautifully clear signal from one to another. When we are 'being' with another person, we haven't got any room left for judging, analysing or solving their problems. There is no space in 'being' to exercise control over someone, to minimise their struggles or quash their dreams. We are simply able to be there with them, alongside them, looking and listening in on their world.

There is something so simple and yet so powerful about 'being', that I find it nearly impossible to fit into words. The unconscious sense and feeling I experience when someone else is 'being' with me is indescribable. I don't sense it in my wordy, logical brain, it is felt deep inside my heart and my gut. When someone else is being with me, I feel something like safe, held, uplifted, worthy, free and important. It gives me a space to express myself that is open and expansive. I so often find myself saying far more than I might ever have imagined, because my companion is fully with me.

Fully Present and in the Moment

Full presence and being in the moment sound straight forward enough, until we realise most of us spend the majority of our time elsewhere in our minds. We may be physically present, but we are seldom mentally, emotionally and spiritually with someone. We often bring part of ourselves into interactions with people, we offer part of our attention, part of our focus and part of our concentration.

Another part of us is elsewhere, thinking, worrying, reflecting, distracted with other thoughts. It is rare we are truly in the moment. We spend so much of our lives planning for the future and reflecting on the past, that we forget to be in the here and now. It is such a simple concept and yet, can prove so tricky to implement. Even as a coach we can find our presence lessened by our concerns over whether the coaching is helping, what question to ask next and the simple wonderings of our own world. I speak with so many people who admit to living their lives already in the next activity. Whatever we are currently doing is only a half-present exercise, because our brain is already preparing for whatever is coming next. We wake in the morning thinking about getting dressed, we get dressed thinking about our breakfast, we eat breakfast thinking about our drive to work, we drive to work thinking about our first task of the day, we do our first task thinking about the next one and so on and so forth all day until we fall asleep, thinking about tomorrow. We have created a culture with very little emphasis on our presence and the moment, yet both of these are vital to the quality of our lives, happiness and relationships. Surprisingly, this ability to be utterly present and in the moment was once our natural state of being. It was once the only way we knew how to be.

Our Greatest Teachers

I am certain there was a time in our lives when we were awesome at being fully present and in the moment. The people in our world who are the greatest at being are the little children around us. We never have to ask a toddler to be in the moment, because they are never anywhere else. They are not thinking about tomorrow or what's happening in an hour's time, they are not replaying conversations in their heads about what went on last month or last year, they are simply being with what is here right now. We never have to ask a toddler to be fully present because they don't understand any other way of being. They are immersed in whatever is happening right now. The good news for all of us then, is that at some point in our lives we were brilliant at being and that ability has never completely left us, it has just perhaps been overshadowed by the busyness and culture of our adult lives. The capacity to 'be' is still in us, it's in all of us and all we need to do is to learn to consciously tap back into it. As a coach we need to take a bit of our toddler self into the coaching relationship with us, to offer our clients our full presence in each and every moment we are with them. Perhaps the best thing we can ever do for another human is not doing at all, but rather being. It is this ability to be that creates a different, richer soil in which people can develop and grow.

Chapter 12

Reality and Improve – Beneath the Surface

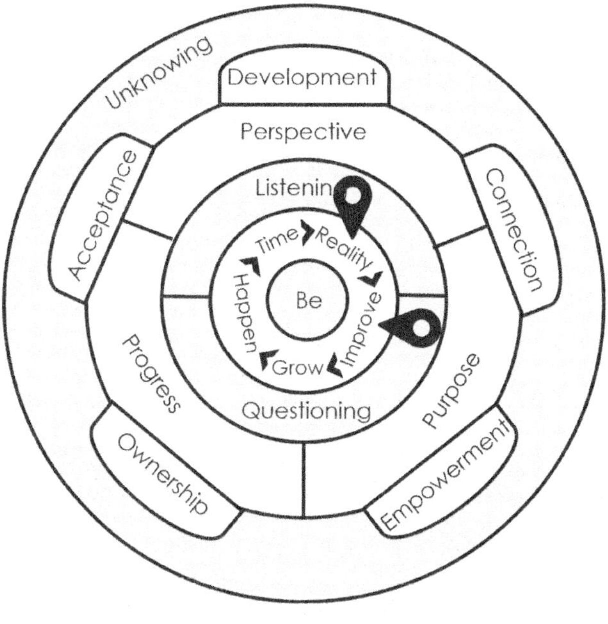

"Reality is merely an illusion, albeit a very persistent one."

Albert Einstein

The Two Realities

"What's happening in your other reality" I tentatively asked. As I awaited an answer, I was still trying to understand the conversation I was embroiled in. I didn't know Stuart very well but sitting in that University coffee lounge listening to him talk about his life with Schizophrenia, was fascinating. I didn't really know how I had ended up there, but it seemed we had in some way, been drawn to each other in the early weeks of our studies and now I was listening to this bright young man, tell me that due to his condition, he always had two different realities going on. He went onto explain that he had the reality that he knew was happening in the real world and then he had the reality he understood to be only happening in his mind.

"Well, in the real world I know that I am Stuart and you are John and we are sitting here at this table drinking coffee, surrounded by other students passing by," he began. "But in my other reality, the one in my mind, you are King Arthur, I am Merlin, we're sat in your court drinking wine and all these people around us are the Knights of the Round Table."

"How often does this happen for you?" I asked

"All the time! In every moment for me, both these realities are happening. But don't worry I don't have a problem with it, as long as I can tell the difference", he assured me. "These two realities don't cause me any difficulties at all as long as I am aware of the difference between them. It's only in the past where I have got them confused, that I ended up getting in trouble."

I was amazed at the time, that a person could live with two different realities and yet I now believe all of us are in some way a bit like Stuart. Not that all of us have Schizophrenia, but rather that we all have our own interpretations of reality going on. Perhaps not as wildly imaginative as Stuart's Camelot, but our own take on reality none the less. Twenty years ago, I'd have laughed at myself writing statements like this and would have told myself that something is either happening or not happening, so therefore there is only one reality, whether people interpret it that way or not. Working closely with all kinds of people over the past two decades, I have experienced the vast interpretations of reality that a single person can be experiencing. It is not so much what is happening that is important; it is how we are interpreting what is happening that truly matters. Our experience of reality is completely subjective and utterly malleable. We need to know this if we are to coach people, because it is imperative to begin by understanding something of their reality from their map of their world, not how that reality sounds, feels or smells in our world.

Starting in a Different Place

John Whitmore said that coaching conversations should always begin with the Goal, which is why his GROW model of coaching follows the pattern of Goal, Reality, Opportunities, Will/Way Forward. When I first began coaching, I was aware of Whitmore's model and tried on numerous occasions to use the GROW model. However, in those days, I was spending a large proportion of my time coaching in schools with teenagers who weren't principally engaged in the education system. Asking these teenagers as my opening gambit, what their goal might be, was frequently met at best with "don't know" and at worst with a fantasy so unrealistic that it made the Lord of Rings look like a fly-on-the-wall documentary.

There is no doubt the GROW model can be useful when working with motivated, ambitious, driven individuals and I hold John Whitmore in the highest esteem for his pioneering work in creating and contributing to the development of coaching. He is one of the giants upon which shoulders all coaches stand. Yet, I quickly discovered for some of my early clients, GROW was beginning in the wrong place for them. They needed to begin with their current interpretation of reality, because that is the only world they knew inside out. I've never yet come across a client who can't describe their present circumstances, or the way in which they are interpreting the world around them. From the youngest child I have ever coached to high-flying Chief Executives, they are all able to show me their world, depict their current understanding of their situation and life. This is the reason my coaching conversations generally begin with discussions about reality and start with the *"what's going on right now for you?"* kind of questions.

Whitmore believes coaching should begin with Goals because of the motivating and inspiring nature of that conversation. I agree with the latter part of this, enabling our clients to be motivated and uplifted, but I believe that firstly we must empower them to explore their starting point, to be aware of what is here in their life, right now. This is so vitally important, because without understanding their reality, I fear many people set off towards a goal that is not necessarily the direction they really want to go in. Exploring reality empowers our clients to gain a deeper awareness of what is really going on for them.

The Surface and Deeper Reality

Although there are varied interpretations of reality happening for people, it is a layered process and people have what I have come to refer to as, a surface reality and a deeper reality. The surface reality is the one our client knows about and is happy to show. The deeper reality is the one they are perhaps, as yet, dimly unaware of. It is crucial as coaches we do not rush our clients through the exploration of their present reality, because if we do, the coaching will only ever remain at a surface level. This means coaching will have some impact, in that it may contribute to the movement of a client from point A in their life to point B, but it lacks any long-lasting growth and development. Spending time with our clients in their reality, empowers them to gain greater understanding of what is really happening for them and enables the coaching to move in a direction of increased importance for them.

I was working with a teacher a few years ago who presented their reality as being over worked, stressed and lacking in any kind of work-life balance. This is sadly a common reality for many within our education system, so it would have been plausible for me to think, 'it's fairly obvious what the problem is, I've worked with this kind of stuff before' and rush off towards the goal of improved work-life balance. If I had done that, I imagine the conversation would have led to discussions around time-management, creating boundaries between home and work and some other kind of strategy to ease the issue. However, I tend not to rush through reality, because I know true awareness of a client's reality for themselves, is an intrinsic part of the growing process. As we discuss and explore a person's reality, their understanding of their own world begins to emerge. On many occasions, they uncover the issue or change they thought they wanted, isn't the real thing at all, it is simply how life is presenting itself on the surface. As I spent time with my teacher client, being curious about what was really going on for him, he began to talk about feeling undervalued by the leadership in the school and in particular, his Head Teacher. He also realised his response to feeling undervalued was to work harder, take on more roles, volunteer for everything and anything that might just get him noticed and ultimately give him some recognition from his leaders. His surface reality was feeling overworked, his deeper reality was being undervalued. I was able to coach around this feeling of being undervalued, help him to explore what being valued might be like, what difference it might make and how he could grow in this area. We never once touched on being overworked again, because that wasn't the issue; it was just how his work was manifesting itself on the surface. By spending time exploring the deeper reality, we are able to coach our clients on the real, important issues. This particular client was able to do two things; firstly shift his own perspective on where he received his sense of value from and secondly go and have a conversation with his Head Teacher about how he was really feeling.

If we only coach the surface reality, we are in danger of ending up just problem solving. Our clients may well get to some kind of action, but it is probably not a long lasting, effective action. The situation will most likely reoccur, perhaps in a different guise, packaged differently, but the same situation none-the-less. When we notice the same patterns occurring in our own or other people's lives, similar issues arising time and again, this is often because it is only being changed temporarily on the surface. The underlying, deeper reality is not progressing, so it repeatedly finds its way back to the surface. I have no interest what-so-ever in short-term temporary change for people, yet if I was to choose to coach only the surface reality, this is what would happen time and again. I wonder how many coaches walk away from their clients at the end of the coaching relationship, patting themselves on the back for their work in helping that client achieve change. Yet blissfully unaware that it is only a temporary shift and perhaps not even the change the client truly wanted, or needed. What I am passionate about is long-lasting, on-going growth and development for people. The kind of movement that only occurs, when people are aware of what is really happening and what is truly important for them. When we discover, with our clients, the deeper reality and coach that, we help empower our clients to find new perspectives and deeper, more effective actions to move forward.

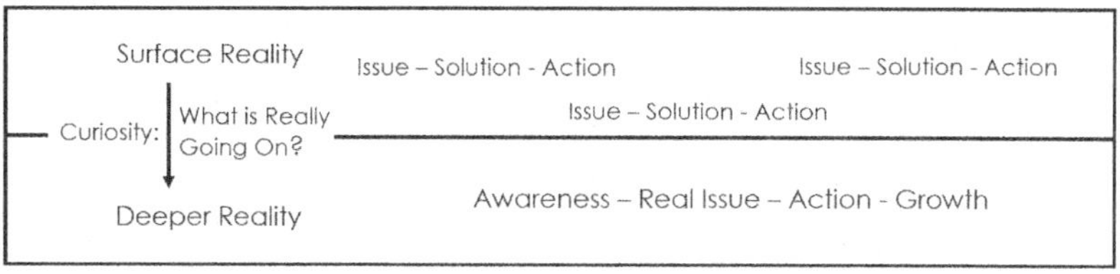

In the deeper reality, I'm not talking about coaching deep psychological issues and I'm not in any way suggesting the coach is taking on the role of some sort of pseudo-psychotherapist or psychoanalyst. If coaching conversations ever delve into those realms, then it is a very clear referral process from the coach to another professional, more equipped to deal with those issues. I am simply suggesting that as coaches we must be curious about our clients' reality. We must be consistent in our wondering of 'what is really going on?' Our clients will wander round all week, having surface conversations with their friends, families and colleagues. When they come to coaching they deserve to be met with a curious coach, who in the interests of the client's growth, is intrigued to help them explore beneath the surface and increase their self-awareness. As coaches we must always be wondering, 'what is truly the reality my client is describing?' Listening for the deeper reality, is a bit like sitting in the theatre. Many clients will simply draw the curtains or just pop out onto stage now and again, but really all they are willing to show us is the parts of them they have learnt are socially acceptable. Others will raise the curtain and allow us to see the performance they have learnt to put on - they will 'show us the show'. However, the job of the coach is to be curious about what is happening 'back-stage', because what is happening back-stage is driving the performance and the reality of our clients. Only when we get back-stage in our clients' lives, are we and they able to see the truer reality and begin to help them to move forward from that place.

Improve

Only once a client begins to understand and make sense of their reality, are they able to truly decide where they would like to make improvements. It is something which often happens naturally within coaching, but at other times needs a specific question to clarify exactly what it is the client wants to improve. It is important to gain some sense of focus within the coaching, some idea of the specific growth our client is looking to make. Other than that, there is very little to say about the focus of a coaching relationship apart from it must come from the client themselves and we must be aware of the life tension involved. Even though a client is choosing to focus the conversation on one particular area, we must always have an eye on how this impacts the bigger picture of their life. Coaching is dangerous when it becomes tunnel vision towards one particular area of improvement and begins to neglect the whole person and the fullness of their life. There is no part of us that lives in isolation from the others and I find no sense of success in coaching a person to fulfil their career ambitions, at the detriment of their family relationships, or coaching a person to achieve their financial vision, at the damage to their health. Culturally, we seem to portray people as huge successes when they have achieved some level of greatness only in one particular area of life. We hold up actors, musicians, entrepreneurs, sports stars and people from a whole host of other fields as successes, even when other parts of their lives fall short of anything we might deem successful. I see success as a holistic entity, where people are able to not only move forward in specific areas of life, but also understand the impact and effect this has on themselves as a whole. It is vital as coaches we help our clients to see the whole spectrum of their life and be curious about how they interplay with one another. Empowering our clients to understand and explore their reality on a deeper level, means they have greater awareness to figure out the focus they want to give and the way they want to move forward.

Chapter 13

Grow - Growth not Goals

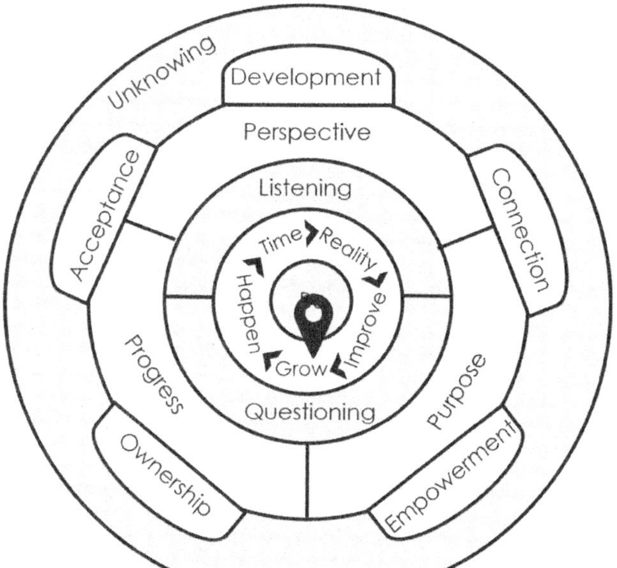

"The problem with reaching the peak of the tallest mountain in your dreams is that the path can only wind down the other side further and further away from this idyllic moment."

Jonny Wilkinson

Losing the Goal

I used to believe at one time people needed goals in their lives to be fully living and yet, I'm not so convinced anymore. I believed once that without goals, life became utterly pointless, like a race with no finishing line or archery with no target but I have come also to see the danger that goals can pose for people, if pursued in isolation.

Jonny Wilkinson was just 9 years old when he set himself the goal of winning the Rugby Union World Cup and he was only 24 years old when he made that happen. With 35 seconds remaining in extra time of the 2003 World Cup Final, the ball was heading from the hands of Matt Dawson into the grasp of Jonny Wilkinson. This was the moment, when all those hours upon hours of kicking practice were to be tested, under the greatest of all pressures. It didn't fail him. Jonny Wilkinson made that infamous drop goal and won the World Cup for England. It's a story that Hollywood itself couldn't write and yet in the minutes and hours that followed, rather than elation and joy, Jonny found himself feeling empty and out of control. *"I had pictured this image – worshipped it even - for years, maybe as long as I could remember. As we walked around the field in our celebratory lap of honour, I could feel my dream beginning to slip away. The brightness was already fading and with each second that passed, so was my happiness."*

How can it be that a young man achieving his life time ambition felt so lost? Because that's exactly it, in winning the World Cup he had also lost; lost the goal that had hung like a guiding star in his life for a decade and a half.

Isolated Goals

Goals lived out in isolation can drive us forward in life, but they can also leave us empty and misplaced once they are achieved. I often come across coaching being described as 'goal oriented' or 'solution focussed'. Yet coaching is actually about growth and development, not goals or solutions. It is "growth-orientated" or "development-focused", because ultimately goals and solutions are only achieved through growth. It is people growing and developing that is at the heart of coaching, not goals. Goals are simply the result of growth. Goals are the achievement part that other people see, they are the pretty flower of coaching not the roots, they are the "good-looking" face, but not the heartbeat. Growing is truly what coaching has to offer people and growth in all its guises, from tiny tweaks to wholesale sweeping developments.

Coaching is often portrayed as a way for people to achieve that promotion, make more income, find that illusive relationship and live some kind of ultimate lifestyle. It seems to be geared toward an array of "goals", that if achieved, will bring greater happiness to the client. However, this feels like such a one-dimensional approach to coaching. I find myself frustrated when coaching is entirely geared towards goals and targets. There is so much potential for growth and only one part (the external achievements) are being tapped. Like using a smart phone only to send texts, coaching has so much more to offer people than just the chance to work towards a goal.

Goals are external targets, they are something to aim for and destinations to reach and they can carry some importance. I have numerous goals in my life and I continually set myself new ones, from weekly ‘run of the mill’ goals to bigger more long-term challenges. At times, goals keep me motivated, excited and enthused for the next chapter of my life, but they are not all that coaching has to offer, they are only a fraction. A lot of coaches seem to really like goals and like working with their clients towards very clear targets. I can see the attraction to this, because they are easy to measure, other people will notice the difference and they look good as case studies on coaching websites. A client achieving a goal makes a coach look like they are doing a great job - and often they are - but there is so much more. Asking people how they want to grow, offers the chance for them to create vision for themselves and vision is vitally important.

Vision

There is a myth that exists within our culture, that suggests we must always have a very clear vision for where we are heading in life and what our goal is, and if we don't know this exactly, we will just wander around never achieving our potential. This is simply one way of doing things, not the only way. It varies from person to person, depending on how we are wired. Some people do have very clear, specific targets. Others are very vague about what exact direction they want to head in. Either of these and anything in between is OK with me, if it works for that person. The danger with having a very specific goal is it leaves very little room for uncertainty and therefore for other possibilities. It places all the emphasis on being there at the goal, rather than on the process and journey. It can create a sense of striving after something, rather than living now. Having said that, vision is really important and I see people struggle when there is no vision at all. However, I don't believe the vision always has to be so exact and so clear it serves to remove all the possibilities and opportunities which might arise. Often, it is more than enough for people to have an idea of the general direction in which they want to move and even just an inkling they want to move somehow and in some way. As people begin to move, grow and develop the vision starts to unfold and become clearer and clearer.

When I was 13 years old, I was on a school football trip abroad. In our second match of the week-long tour, a thunderbolt of a shot smacked me at close range, slap bang in my right eye. My eye bled internally. It filled with blood so much that my iris wasn't even visible, it was just this big swelling ball of red in my eye socket. At first, I couldn't see anything through it, just complete darkness. I remember on the way to the hospital, feeling the fear that I had lost my sight in that eye. By the time we got to the hospital though, I was beginning to see some shadowy figures right in front of me. When I closed my left eye, as the doctor asked me to do, I knew the he was stood in front of me. I could see a shape move around a bit, but I couldn't see outlines or colours, or any clear definition at all. Over the next few days, as the blood started to drain from my eye, it began to feel as though I was peering through a net curtain, until thankfully over the following weeks and months my sight fully returned.

The feeling of being only able to see outlines, feels a bit like many of my clients looking at their futures. They kind of know where they want to head but can't see any of the details. Some can only see shadowy shapes in front of them, others are peering at their futures through a net curtain and only a handful come to coaching with a detailed vision. Even when they do, they often discover it's not quite as clear as they perhaps first thought.

It is not wrong or uncommon to not have clearly defined goals, or to not even know your goals at all. It is much more about the growth and development that people want to make, the progress they want to create and the journey they are on. Goals are all about the destination, whereas growing is about the journey and the process.

It's like setting off on a pirate voyage to find Treasure Island. If we were to do so, we would chart a course and set sail in the right direction. We would ensure we were always moving forward and always heading the right way. But as we were setting sail, we wouldn't have a very clear picture of what the island actually looked like. We would probably have a map that gave us the outline and a few sketchy details. We would know it was over the horizon somewhere and we would set off towards it. We would have no way of knowing the exact details of the island. Only as we got much closer and the island appeared on the horizon, would we have our first glimpse of our goal. Even then it wouldn't be a detailed view, just probably a dark, blurry spot. As we move closer and closer the more detailed the picture would become and still only when we landed and set foot on the island, would we see its full detail. Any goals we have are very much like this, because so much of what is to come is simply unknown.

The Danger of Goals

There are dangers to having a specific goal that are rarely mentioned. Firstly, there is a danger of missing opportunities because it doesn't fit with our exact plan. Imagine the pirates setting off to Treasure Island, with a clear detailed picture. On their way, they sail passed another island with a treasure chest full of gold and silver sitting right there on the beach. They perhaps don't even see it, because they are so focused on the destination, or they consciously choose to ignore it and keep sailing past because it's not the 'right' island.

Secondly, it's dull and takes the fun out of the future. Part of the beauty of the future, is its mystery. We should plan and think and dream of our futures, but we should be open to the opportunities of what the future might present. That is the richness and adventure of life for us humans. If we control every single detail, we lose the sense of adventure along the way and as we already know, we can't control every single detail anyway. Knowing every detail spoils the thrill of the journey. I travelled once from Vancouver up to Whistler in Western Canada. It was the most amazing, beautiful journey I've ever been on. It was simply breath-taking, and I loved every minute of it. Every corner we journeyed round threw up a new jaw-droppingly, picture perfect, landscape of mountains and fjords. I never wanted that journey to end. A few days later, I was talking to one of the ski instructors who worked up in Whistler. He was from Vancouver and he regularly travelled up and down to there. I told him I thought he had the best commute in the world. His reply was one of melancholy "Well", he said, "it's still a commute and it gets boring when you've done it as much as I have". The most amazing journey I had ever been on, to him was just a commute. The difference was simple. I didn't know what to expect round each bend. I knew where we were heading. I had seen pictures of Whistler, I had a rough idea what it would be like, but I had no idea of the details of the journey, I was full of anticipation and wonder. The ski instructor on the other hand, knew every single detail, every turn, every fjord, every mountain peak and that comprehensive knowledge created boredom for him.

Thirdly, on occasions people will present specific goals that are not goals at all, but rather fantasies. They are goals that cannot possibly happen. This may be because they are outside of the law of physics, they are a completely random event, or they are well beyond a client's abilities and reach. It is important not to dismiss these fantasies out of hand, but rather to become curious about what growth this fantasy represents. What is underpinning the fantasy? I have worked with a number of teenage boys who tell me their goal is to play football for Manchester United and yet the reality is, they aren't even getting picked for their school football team.

This isn't a goal for them, it is a fantasy. This obviously varies from person to person, because I have also worked with a few teenage boys who are now playing professional football and do have a chance, if things go their way, of playing football at that level. However, it is important for me to never dismiss people's fantasies, but rather to spend time with them discovering what that fantasy represents and what growth they are wanting to make. Perhaps, for them, it is about feeling successful, receiving recognition or finding a job they will love. If we are only working with goals we would have to dismiss the fantasy out of hand, because it is unachievable, but when we see coaching as a way of helping people to grow, then fantasies can become a useful part of that process.

More than Goals

Goals most definitely have their place, but coaching human development is so much more about the possibilities of how we are going to grow, rather than the specific of living from one goal to another. Carl Rogers summed it up brilliantly when he said *"Life, at its best, is a flowing, changing process in which nothing is fixed. In my clients and myself I find when life is richest and most rewarding it is a flowing process. To experience this is both fascinating and a little frightening. I find I am at my best when I can let the flow of my experience carry me, in a direction which appears to be forward, toward goals of which I am but dimly aware."*

Chapter 14

Happen and Time – The Call to Action

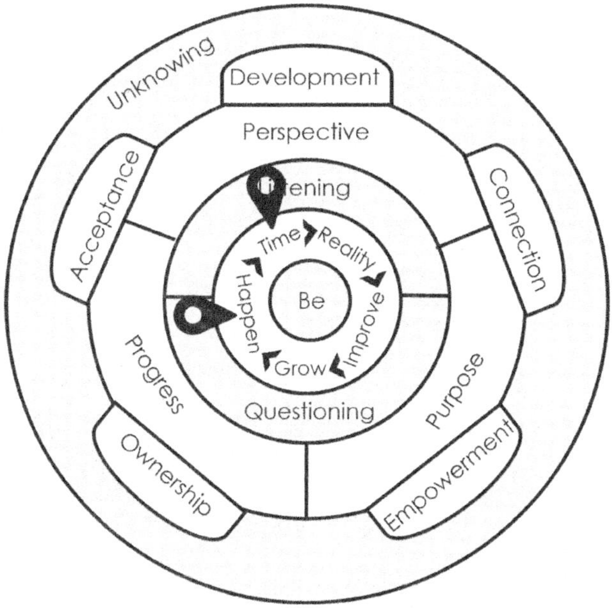

"The more often he feels without acting, the less he will be able ever to act, and, in the long run, the less he will be able to feel."

C.S. Lewis, The Screwtape Letters

Making a Living Happen

In order for growth to occur there must at some point be some action or difference in behaviour. We must put all of the talk into practice. Otherwise the talk remains just that, talk. As great as talk is, it doesn't, by itself, complete the process of growth.

When I started out at the very beginning of this journey, I didn't know that setting up a coaching business was supposed to be a difficult process. Not knowing that, was the most helpful thing of all. Towards the end of my training programme, I was involved in a conference call with my fellow trainees and our mentor. The session involved discussion around our development, next steps and the building of a coaching practice. Our mentor asked us to tell the group how many practice coaching sessions we had done, how many clients we were regularly working with and how many of those had started paying for our services. We began to go around the group of about twenty, from all corners of Europe. As each person took turns to share their answers to the questions, it gradually dawned on me that I hadn't quite been doing what everyone else seemed to have been doing. Many people were saying they had done up to a maximum of 10 practice sessions, perhaps had 1 or 2 ongoing clients and the odd person had a client or two who was actually paying for the service. When it became my turn to share my answers, I was consumed with embarrassment.

My answers felt so different from what I had heard, that I began to doubt myself. I wanted to soften my response for fear of standing out from the crowd, though I had no choice but to tell the truth.

"I've done between 50 and 60 first time sessions, I have 12 ongoing clients and 10 of those are currently paying various amounts depending on their start date with me."

Darren responded first, *"Sorry John, did you say you've done over 50 first time sessions? How on earth have you done that?"*

I stumbled, *"Err, I don't really know. I kind of thought that's how many we were all doing!"*

He pressed me, *"But where have you found those people from, how have you had so many people who have had a session with you in such a short space of time? How have you got that many paying clients? What have you done?"*
At this point I could feel the weight of expectation, as if I was going to reveal a huge secret about how to build a coaching practice. The problem was that I didn't know what the secret was, so I just went with my story.

I didn't think I knew anything about business, I had never run a business before and never undertaken any studies in it whatsoever. However, what I discovered in the discussion that followed was, I had managed to build the beginnings of a successful coaching business by simply and innocently talking to people about coaching. I had never once tried to sell my services. I had unknowingly 'waxed lyrical' about coaching and all its benefits to anyone that cared to listen. In answer to the question, where I had found all these coaching clients from, I realised the absurdity of my answer. I think people were expecting me to reveal some funky marketing plan or creative PR campaign, but the reality of my answer was as far removed from that as could be.

"A couple of my coaching clients I met at a barbeque, one of them I sat next to on a train, another I spoke to for a few minutes by the pool on holiday, a lot of them are friends of friends, or friends of colleagues… I don't really know where I've found them."

I hadn't been looking for coaching clients, I had just wanted to tell the world how amazing I thought coaching was and offer people a chance to experience it. It seemed people had bought into it. I was aware when I met new people, they would inevitably ask me what I did for a living and somewhere along the line, I had stopped telling people about my day job and started telling people I was training to be a coach.

I assumed, like me, once people knew what coaching was, they would obviously want to try it. I wasn't het up with ideas of how to build a successful coaching business or what might happen if I fail. I thought of everyone as a potential coaching client and I wanted as much practice as I could get. I would go to work all day, then come home and coach people. It wasn't a chore, I loved it.

I found out that while I had been gathering clients, the majority of my peers had been thinking about their businesses, getting their branding and websites ready for launch, planning and strategizing over their business plans and pondering a whole load of other things that weren't actually coaching. I, on the other hand, had been doing none of that, I had inadvertently been getting on with making things happen, taking action and driving my ambitions forward. I could have talked and thought all day long, about building a coaching business, but that doesn't actually build anything. Like everything else, it needs thought and talk but in the end in needs action.

A few years later a friend of mine went through the same training course I had done. He told me that during a session about how to build a coaching practice, the mentor told a story of a guy she had worked with, who built a practice in double-quick time by doing nothing more than talking about coaching to anyone who would listen. I didn't know I wasn't meant to.

STAR Actions

In my early coaching days, when my clients began to talk about what actions they were going to take to move forward, I initially related it to the renowned process of SMART Targets. I'd be checking in to see if their actions were Specific, Measurable, Achievable, Realistic and Timed, and in this way, I felt I would be able to hold them accountable to their progress. Over the years, this thinking has developed somewhat for me and although I still hold accountability with my clients, I think about actions in a slightly different way. What has emerged is a way of reflecting on my clients' actions and behaviours through a series of four simple questions that have become an internal checklist for me. To make them memorable, I have nick-named these STAR Actions, because the four questions I ask of my clients' actions are: -

Is it **S**tretching?

Is it within their **T**ime Bubble?

Is it **A**ccountable?

Is it **R**esonating?

Is it Stretching?

Aaron Fotheringham was 8 years old when he wheeled himself onto the skate park for the first time. He had been sitting and watching his older brother perform tricks and stunts from behind the fence for some time, but he had never had a go himself until this moment. But then, who would have thought that an 8-year-old boy with Spina Bifida, paralysed from the waist down would have the courage to venture out onto the Skate Park and start riding around in his wheelchair. It was the beginning of something incredible, yet almost inconceivable. Aaron didn't stop there, he started to practice stunts and tricks, falling and failing time and again. He broke his elbow, smashed his face and broke his wheelchair, but time and again, he would dust himself down and go again. He never once returned to watching from the safety of behind the fence. At the age of 15, Aaron went on to become the first person in the world to successfully perform a backflip in a wheelchair. The video of this world first was posted on the internet and within days it went viral. Aaron Fotheringham had become an inspiration to millions. It started, because he had the courage to move out from behind the fence, from the safety zone, into an area of risk and danger; and he has just kept pushing his boundaries ever since. At 19 years old, Aaron become the first person in the world to land a double back flip in a wheelchair. Whenever it seemed that he could relax now and play it safe, revel in his success, he has stretched himself again and again. Nobody would have blamed that 8-year-old boy for staying behind that fence, for watching from the side-lines and keeping himself safe. Yet because of his courage and strength to step past his fears, he has experienced a risky life, one full of physical injury and danger, but also bursting with fulfilment, excitement and wonder.

I wonder whether there was something about Aaron's age that helped him to take the risk and go out onto that skate park for the first time. I wonder if he was teenager, or in his twenties, or thirties at the time, whether he would have taken the same risk. Whether the desire to "play it safe" would have been stronger in him and he would have been content to sit and watch. We all have the ability to step beyond our fears and take some risks, but over the years it perhaps gets knocked out of us, or worry so consumes us, we believe the better option is to play it safe. Perhaps it's our survival instinct in overdrive that we want to prolong our life, so everything we do is geared towards safety and security. There is a problem with too much safety, security and comfort, because it can start to impact on our confidence, fulfilment and development. In order to grow there is a certain amount of risk and discomfort we need and we have to find the strength to stretch ourselves and push ourselves forward.

I first came across the idea of people not only having a comfort zone but also a stretch and panic zone in Susan Jefferies best seller, “Feel the Fear and Do It Anyway”. The more time I have spent working with people around growth, the more obvious it has become to me just how much we humans love our comfort zones and often try and dodge our stretch and panic zones at all costs. We are so often unaware of our comfort zone, because it is the place where anything we are doing, anyone we are with or anywhere we are, makes us feel completely comfortable. In another sense, we are so at ease, we don’t think twice about it. Our stretch zone is the place where whatever we are doing, anyone we are with or anywhere we are, makes us feel like we are having to stretch ourselves to do it. It might be a big stretch or a little stretch, but it often involves “butterflies in our stomach”, a fear or worry of some kind, or a sense of being out of our depth. Our stretch zone is the place where it is still possible for us to accomplish certain things, but we may well need a lot of support, encouragement, or a strong enough reason to do it. Our panic zone is the place where anything we are doing, anyone we are with or anywhere we are, sends us into a complete panic. It is our fight, flight or freeze place. We will fight, run away or completely clam up to get out of the situation. It is where our fears often become irrational and we are sent into an internal frenzy.

The reason for checking which zone the action my clients are committing to, is in, is because quite simply, there is no growing that gets done in our comfort zone and there is no helpful experience that occurs in our panic zones. Our stretch zones are the only place in which real growing takes place and if we are serious about developing, then we must be prepared to step out into our stretch zones. Development isn't created in our comfort zone, because we can already accomplish everything in there with ease. We are 100% confident in our own abilities in our comfort zones, so there is no growing to be done there. Development isn't created in our panic zones either, because if we are forced into doing things in our panic zone, the experience is so overwhelmingly terrifying, we often promise ourselves we will never do it again. Our panic zone can effectively put us off for life. The only place growth takes place is in our stretch zone. When we are able to step out of our comfort zone and take action that is in our stretch zone, we are effectively pushing the walls of our comfort zone outwards. We are starting the process of growing. As coaches it is vital we empower our clients to set actions for themselves that are within their stretch zones and help them readjust if they are playing it safe in their comfort zone or chunk it down if they are driving themselves into their panic zones.

Is it in their Time Bubble?

When I first decided to start a coaching business, I was told that I needed a five-year business plan. I had absolutely no idea about business and therefore thought this must be right, so I set about writing a five-year plan. Now here's the problem with that. I struggle to see clearly what five years from now looks like. I can see it in part, but not in great detail. I don't really live in five-year sections. Asking me what five-years from now looks like, is a bit like asking me to imagine the year 3000. I could give you a few suggestions about what life may be like then, but the truth is, there are so many conceivable differing outcomes, that it becomes a bit blurry. I could make a load of suggestions about what the possibilities may be, but it's so far away for me, it almost feels like I'm talking about a fantasy. That's because we all have these things I like to call 'Time Bubbles'. Our 'Time Bubble' is simply the amount of time, either side of our present moment, that we can really conceive. It's the amount of time that truly feels real to us.

When we were small children our 'Time Bubble' was measured in seconds, rather than minutes. Explaining to a toddler they are going on holiday in a month's time, is just like saying "you are off on holiday in 100 years". Their concept of time is miniscule, and they can see only a moment into the future. Hence the infamous *"are we nearly there yet?"* two minutes into a six-hour car journey. They have no concept of it. As a teenager, we could possibly see a bit further ahead and our time bubble was bigger, but it probably only got us to the weekend, or perhaps the end of the school term. I speak with a lot of teenagers in their last year of school and even though they know they are leaving school in a matter of months, they still struggle to really believe it is going to happen. Most teenagers can often picture clearly the week or fortnight ahead, but much further than that and everything gets a bit foggy for them. Often adults will ask teenagers what they want to be when they grow up, but the reality is asking the average teenager what they what to be when they grow up is like asking me what nursing home I'd like to be in when I'm 95 years old. I honestly can't really visualise being 95 years old. I hope I live to be that age, but I can't really imagine my life then. If actions exist outside of our Time Bubble they don't feel real and we struggle to find any motivation to do them. We will only start to truly act upon our goals once they enter our Time Bubbles. For example, if a 20-year-old's goal is to be a millionaire by the time they are 40, but their Time Bubble is only one year long, they will do nothing about becoming a millionaire until they are 39 years old and by then there probably isn't enough time left to make it a reality.

I began to realise my Time Bubble varies for different parts of my life. In business, it is generally about 6 to 18 months long; where as in my personal life, I tend to live more month to month. I can clearly see how I want to achieve my business aims over the next year or so, but past that the vision becomes foggy. I can see how my personal life looks over the next few months but again, after that it is blurry. Everyone's Time Bubble is unique and each person can cope with and visualize, different periods of time. It's perfectly okay if our and our client's long-term vision is a bit fuzzy because as we know it doesn't need to have all the details. Due to our Time Bubbles, the closer an event is to us, the clearer our vision of it is. So, for example, if we were asked to visualise what we are doing tomorrow, I'm certain we would be able to describe our day in full detail. If we were asked about a day next month, we would probably have a good idea what our day might look like. What about describing a day a year from now, or a day 10 or 20 years from now? The further away it gets, the blurrier our vision of it becomes. It is perfectly okay if longer-term goals don't have all the details attached to it yet; but actions must sit firmly within our Time Bubbles otherwise we will not be motivated enough to get them done.

When I sat down to write my five-year business plan, I could see some very clear targets and actions for the first year, but after that it was a bit of a blur and to be honest I made up years 2 to 5. Setting actions outside of our 'Time Bubble' is a pointless exercise, because we can't truly buy into them as something that will really happen. We struggle to believe in them, to believe they can be our reality and because they are outside of our Time Bubbles, we ignore them until the passage of time causes them to enter it. We can have goals and visions that sit outside our Time Bubble, like the idea that "one day I will do this..." or "by the time I'm 50 years old I'd like..." but our actions must be within them. We are only motivated and stirred to action by things that are within our Time Bubbles. We must be checking in with our clients' Time Bubble and asking whether the actions they are talking about fit within them. If they don't, we can then discuss what stepping stones in the nearer future might they need first. I often speak with my clients about what actions they are looking to achieve within the next week or month, because for most people this places the action firmly within their Time Bubble.

Is it Accountable?

Accountability is vital in the process of growth. Having another human being who will walk alongside us and hold us to account, is both motivating and reassuring in equal measure. Having said that though, we love and hate accountability, all at the same time. We want to have someone to be accountable to, but we often try and duck out of being accountable to anyone, because we know that accountability demands something from us.

The best example of the power of accountability is found within the weight loss industry. At venues all over the western world people pay money and queue up, to be weighed by someone else. People believe they are paying for the diet program or the low-fat products, when in fact more than that, they are paying for accountability. There is a plethora of knowledge around what a person needs to eat and not eat to lose weight and how best to combine that with exercise. We can all buy some scales and weigh ourselves in the comfort of our own homes. Yet thousands choose every week to be weighed by someone else. This is the power of accountability. Having someone else who will check in with us and celebrate our successes with us whilst also exploring with us, what got in the way. Having someone who doesn't let us off the hook or buy into our excuses for not doing or achieving what we really wanted to achieve, is powerful

I hold my clients accountable in a similar way and when they are setting themselves an action, I am always checking whether that action is accountable or not. Often clients will set a vague action for themselves such as 'being more confident' or 'thinking positively'. As great as these decisions are, they are impossible to be held to account on. As a coach I have no way of knowing whether my client has been *more confident* or *thought positively*, so I cannot truly hold them accountable to these actions. If I'm ever presented with these types of actions from my clients, I become curious about how they will know they have done this? What will being *more confident* or *thinking positively* actually look like? What will they notice? What will others notice? And how will I, as their coach, know they have achieved this? In this way it creates an accountable action and accountability is vital to the success and impact of coaching.

Is it Resonating?

In our modern western culture, we often like to pride ourselves in our ability to be logical, whilst at the same time playing down any emotion involved. Sadly, we often see reason as a strength and emotion as a weakness. Yet it is emotion that drives us, more than logic. Marketeers know this full well, which is why most advertisements are not aimed at our logic, but rather at our emotions. Businesses know we are rarely motivated to buy by our logic, we are motivated by our emotions. If we were logical creatures, then charity events like Children in Need or Comic Relief would be two minutes in length. The presenter would come on and explain to us logically that children are suffering, we have some spare cash and that money will really help. We would then all logically give our spare cash to the charity and that would be that. However, the fundraisers know they need to find a way to help us to connect emotionally with the cause, with the people involved and only when we are emotionally motivated will we part with our cash. The same is true for any action or growth a human is going to make, there must be something about it that is emotionally resonating, or we won't ever get around to making it happen.

Unless the actions my clients are looking to take are resonating emotionally with them, it is unlikely they will ever experience enough desire and motivation to make them happen. This doesn't mean they are thrilled by every action, there are a plethora of emotions they may be feeling from fear to sadness, to anger to excitement. It is simply important that they are feeling something, and the action is resonating with them in some way. When something is resonating we will notice it. It might be in the form of tears or smiles, clenched fists or fidgeting in their chair, but we will see something going on for our clients and it's important we notice and listen to what is and isn't resonating with them. It's vital that actions are resonating with our clients, because without it there is little motivation and things simply won't happen. If I ever notice an action doesn't seem to be resonating, I will check in with my client and then simply explore further the reasons for that.

Coaching Actions

Although we never know what actions are best for our clients, it is important we journey with them in the process of figuring this out. We won't ever set the actions for them, but we will be there to aid them in the fine tuning of them. By checking out whether our clients' actions are stretching, in time bubbles, accountable and resonating, it empowers them to hone and refine the actions and behaviours they are setting themselves and gives them greater clarity around the onward journey of their growth. It isn't an exact science and it never should be, it is simply a guideline for coaches in helping clients to set very personalised and purposeful actions for themselves.

Epilogue

No Right, No Wrong

Who Knows?

"Am I getting coaching right?", "I feel like I'm getting it all wrong!", "I've just had a really bad session with a client!" These are all comments I have heard countless times from trainee coaches desperate for reassurance they are getting it right, or at least, not getting it wrong. All these statements remind me of a story, a parable I heard years ago that helps capture a broader thinking on the issue of right or wrong and good or bad. It is a tale that originates from the ancient Chinese philosophical and religious tradition of Taoism.

There was a farmer and one day his horse ran off, so the farmer's neighbour came over to commiserate him on his bad luck. The farmer responded by asking, "Who knows what is good or bad?" This confused the neighbour somewhat as the horse was the farmer's prized possession.

But the next day the horse came back and brought with him other wild horses, so the neighbour came over again to congratulate the farmer on his good fortune, to which the farmer responded again, "Who knows what is good or bad?"

The next day the farmer's son tried to ride one of the wild horses to break it in, but instead fell off and broke his own leg. The neighbour appeared again to offer his sympathies to the farmer. The farmer responded a third time with, "Who knows what is good or bad?"

A day later and the army came to the farmer's village looking to conscript the fit, young men. They took one look at the farmer's son and spared him because of his broken leg.

Many times, within my early coaching career I felt like the neighbour in this story. Seeing everything in black or white, good or bad, right or wrong. I would feel like coaching sessions had gone well or gone badly, I would feel like I had done it right or got it wrong. I would feel like I had been great for one client and terrible for another.
Yet, we could retell this same story in a coaching sense.

It's the story of a coach, who had worked with a client for months, but the client didn't appear to be making any progress. The coach's neighbour came over to commiserate the coach on her 'wrong' coaching. The coach responded by asking, "Who knows what is right or wrong?" This confused the neighbour somewhat as making a difference to clients was the coach's main concern.

But the next month the same client referred three colleagues for coaching because they felt coaching had helped them so much. The neighbour came over again to congratulate the coach on her 'right' coaching, to which the coach responded again, "Who knows what is right or wrong?"

The next month the coach started sessions with one of the new clients, but the client didn't book in for further sessions and never got back in touch with the coach. The neighbour appeared again to offer his sympathies to the coach on her 'wrong' coaching. The coach responded a third time with, "Who knows what is right or wrong?"

A year later, the coach got an email from the same client offering them a big contract with a company they now work at, because they remembered the impact of that initial coaching session.

I much prefer now to be the farmer in the first story and have the same attitude the coach in the second story holds. To not know what is right or wrong, good or bad is an imperative perspective to hold as a coach, because if we are needing to know whether we are doing it right or getting it wrong we have left the unknown and started working in an analytical way; looking at our own performance and assessing it against some made-up measures we might have for ourselves. Our incessant desire to be *right* and perhaps even more powerfully *not wrong* is the main thing that gets in the way of us being able to be in the unknowing. It's the stumbling block I see occur over and over again in our coach training courses, people needing to know whether they are doing it right or whether they're getting it wrong. I can't emphasise this enough, there is no right or wrong within coaching. There is just the best we have in that moment with our client. The only time we can speak of right or wrong is within an ethical sense, other than that, there is just what we have to offer at that time and place. We could perhaps have heard something different, asked an alternative question or responded in another way, but none of this makes it right or wrong, it's just different. In any interaction with anyone, there is a multitude of parallel conversations that could have happened, like a tree of life branching out with each response. However, who's to ever know whether a different interaction would have been better or worse. There is simply what is happening and so long as we are committed to offering our clients the best we have, then there can never be a right or wrong. To be great at coaching, we must be able to put away thoughts of good or bad, right or wrong. In doing so we are putting away the conditioning of our entire education system, so this may take some time to master, but it is imperative that we do. So often we were praised in our upbringing for being right and scolded for being wrong, that we developed a very black and white view of the world, which can be hard to shake off. We must find a way, otherwise we will find ourselves on such a rollercoaster ride in our coaching it will be exhausting.

I have seen many coaches attempting to analyse whether their coaching is good or bad, by looking at the progress their clients make. When their clients make progress, they consider themselves a good coach and when their clients stall, they believe they are struggling as a coach. I find this so flawed, because I have had clients who were so ready to make progress they could have had coaching with the world's worst coach and still moved forward. I have also had clients who could have had coaching from the greatest coach there has ever been, and they would have still only inched forward. To assess the quality of our coaching based purely on what our clients do or don't do is dangerous, because "who knows what is good or bad?" What might be right in one moment with one client; might be wrong in another moment with a different client. Whether or not something is good or bad, right or wrong is so personal that the only person capable of answering that to any extent, is the client themselves. They are the only person qualified enough to give any opinion on whether the coaching is helpful or unhelpful for them in that moment, and even then, they may not like something in the moment that later they discover to be really useful. We must learn to trust the process and trust ourselves to simply offer the best we have to our clients. If we are doing that, then we can do no more.

The irony is that whilst we are concerned with being right or wrong, we are taking our focus off '*being*' with our client and therefore missing the very heart beat of coaching itself. We have made it about our performance and not about the connection. We must learn to let it go and be with 'unknowing' in all its guises, including whether we are right or wrong. Let's embrace not-knowing and let the wonder of that place unravel before us as we journey with people in their worlds to places as yet unknown.

The End

Acknowledgements

There are a multitude of people I need to thank who have contributed to the ideas and thoughts in this book and if I was to mention each individual involved, I would be able to fill a whole other book. Some of them are the names you will find in my references, whose writings have influenced and inspired me. Some are my colleagues who over the years have endlessly talked with me and helped me hone and shape my thinking. Some are my coaching clients and those I have trained who continuously challenged me to improve my coaching. Some are my friends who have simply supported and loved me.

However, there are a few individuals who do deserve a special mention. My business partner Jayne Chudley, who has shared this crazy journey with me. My parents for asking me questions when I was child, rather than giving me answers. Zoe Butler, for going the extra mile to get the imagery we needed. Yvonne Hemmings for sorting all the details out. Michelle Richardson for reading and re-reading to the point where you knew it by heart. My three kids, who at the present don't even really understand what I do, but I hope one day this book will make sense to you. Lastly, my wife Rachel, all of this is only possible because you are and always will be my hero.

Thank you one and all.

References and Sources

Books

Albom, Mitch. *Tuesdays with Morrie*. Doubleday, 1997.

Berne, Eric. *Games People Play*. Reserve (s).

Board, Robert de. *Counselling for Toads: a psychological adventure*. Routledge, 2017.

Covey, Stephen R. *7 Habits of Highly Effective People*. Simon & Schuster ltd, 2013.

Crompton, Margaret. *Children and Counselling*. E. Arnold, 1992.

Dahl, Roald. *The BFG*. Scholastic Ltd., 2017.

Frankl, Viktor E., et al. *Man's Search for Meaning*. Beacon Press, 2017.

Grosz, Stephen. *The Examined Life*. Vintage Books, 2014.

Hamilton, Bethany. *Soul Surfer: a True Story of Faith, Family, and Fighting to Get Back on the Board*. Pocket Books, 2012

Hargreaves, Roger. *Mr Men*. Egmont, 2013.

Holy Bible, New International readers Version, Biblica, 2014.

Jeffers, Susan J. *Feel the Fear and Do It Anyway*. Vermilion, 2013.

Kimsey-House, Henry et al. *Co-Active Coaching: New Skills for Coaching People toward Success in Work and Life*. Davies-Black Pub, 2009.

Kipling, Rudyard. *The Light That Failed*. Sydney Industrial Blind Institute, 1926.

Kline, N. *Time to Think*. Cassell Illustrated, 1999.

Lewis, C. S. *The Four Loves*. HarperOne, 2017.

Lewis, C. S. *The Lion, the Witch and the Wardrobe*. Harper, 2009.

Lewis, C. S. *The Screwtape Letters*. CrossReach Publications, 2016.

Luxmoore, Nick. *Feeling like Crap: Young People and the Meaning of Self-Esteem*. Jessica Kingsley Publishers, 2008.
Mearns, Dave, et al. *Person-Centred Counselling in Action*. SAGE, 2013.
Meyer, Erin. *The Culture Map*. PublicAffairs.
Neill, Michael. *The inside-out Revolution: the Only Thing You Need to Know to Chance Your Life Forever*. Hay House, 2013.
Parrado, Nando. *Miracle in the Andes: 72 Days on the Mountain and My Long Trek Home*. Weidenfeld & Nicolson, 2018.
Peck, M. Scott. *The Road Less Travelled*. Rider, 2012.
Peters, Steve. *The Chimp Paradox*. Vermilion, an Imprint of Ebury Publishing, 2016.
Powell, John. *The Secret of Staying in Love: Loving Relationships through Communication*. Allen, 1974.
Prever, Mark. *Counselling and Supporting Children and Young People: a Person-Centred Approach*. SAGE, 2010.
Rogers, Carl. *On Becoming a Person: A Therapist's View of Psychotherapy*. Constable. 1961.
Rogers, Carl. *A Way of Being*. Houghton Mifflin. 1980.
Rogers, Carl. *Carl Rogers Reader* edited by Kirschenbaum, Howard. Constable And Robinson, 1990.
Rowling, J. K. *Harry Potter and the Chamber of Secrets*. Bloomsbury, 2016.
Spinelli, Ernesto. *The Interpreted World: an Introduction to Phenomenological Psychology*. Sage, 2011
Starr, Julie. *The Coaching Manual*. Pitman Publishing, 2010.
Tolhurst, Judith. *The Essential Guide to Coaching and Mentoring*. Longman, 2010.
Tolkien, J. R. R. *Fellowship of the Ring*. HarperCollins Publishers Limited, 2015.
Tolle, Eckhart. A New Earth. Penguin, 2016.

Whitmore, John. *Coaching for Performance: Growing People, Performance and Purpose*. Nicholas Brealey Publishing, 2004.
Wilkinson, Jonny, and Steve Black. *Tackling Life: Striving for My Type of Perfection*. Headline, 2009.
Zondervan. *Serenity Prayer: Reflections and Scripture on the Serenity Prayer*. Zondervan, 2014.

Films

Alive: The Miracle of the Andes. Frank Marshall, Director. Buena Vista Pictures 1993.
Big. Penny Marshall, Director. 20th Century Fox,1988.
Hook. Steven Spielberg, director. TriStar Pictures, 1991.
Soul Surfer. Sean McNamara, Director. Film District & TriStar Pictures, 2011.

Songs

Minchin, Tim. Naughty: Matilda the musical, 2011
Williams, Michelle. Tightrope, The Greatest Showman Soundtrack, 2018

Websites

Einstein, Albert. *Goodreads*, 2018 www.goodreads.com/quotes/search?utf8=%E2%9C%93%2Calbert%2Beinstein%2Breality.
Ferroni, Nicholas. *Flippen Group*, 29 Nov. 2016. www.flippengroup.com/for-too-many-students-school-is-the-one-place-they-receive-love/.
Jung, Carl. *Goodreads*, 2018 www.goodreads.com/quotes/search?utf8=%E2%9C%93%2Cthe%2Bmost%2Bterrifying%2Bthing

Marsh, Michael K. "Divinity Hidden." *Interrupting the Silence*, 25 May 2009. www.interruptingthesilence.com/2009/05/25/divinity-hidden/.

Segovia, Andres. *Brainy Quote*, Xplore, 2018 www.brainyquote.com/authors/andres_segovia.

Singer, Penny. "REMEMBER LIBERTY'S SCAFFOLD?" *The New York Times*, The New York Times, 6 July 1986, www.nytimes.com/1986/07/06/nyregion/remember-liberty-s-scaffold.html.

Yogi, Sahaj. *Farmers Son: A Wisdom Tale*, 2018 www.rainbowbody.com/newarticles/farmerson.htm.